YEATS AND MAGIC: THE EARLIER WORKS

YEATS AND MAGIC: THE EARLIER WORKS

Mary Catherine Flannery

Irish Literary Studies 2

Copyright © 1977 by Colin Smythe Ltd.

Published in the U.S.A. 1978 by Harper & Row Publishers, Inc. Barnes & Noble Import Division

ISBN 0–06–492102–6
LC No. 77–244

Produced in Great Britain

Do
    Jonathan
Mo Céad Leabair

Contents

INTRODUCTION 5

ACKNOWLEDGEMENTS 9

CHAPTER

   I. REVERIES, THEOSOPHY AND CABBALISM: THE EARLY YEARS 11

   II. YEATS AND BLAKE: THE BEGINNINGS OF CONFIDENCE AND OF A SYSTEM 37

   III. YEATS AND IRELAND: THE SEARCH FOR AN IDENTITY THROUGH POLITICS, MAGIC AND MYTHOLOGY . . 53

   IV. MYTHOLOGY AND RITUALS: THE MOVEMENT THROUGH 'HODOS CHAMELIONTOS' TOWARD SYNTHESIS . . 79

   V. MAGIC AND POETRY: THE PATH FROM ASSERTION OF BELIEF TO CONFRONTATION OF THE ANTI-SELF AND THE BEGINNINGS OF RESPONSIBILITY . . . 107

SELECTED BIBLIOGRAPHY 149

INDEX 161

Introduction

William Butler Yeats died on Saturday, 28 January 1939. About a week before that date, he had said to Dorothy Wellesley, 'I feel I am only beginning to understand how to write'.[1] Constantly criticizing, rethinking and revising his works, Yeats was always unsatisfied with his past achievement. He stated his sense of beginning to understand how to write at regular intervals, and as the record of his published and unpublished manuscripts shows, no writer was ever more concerned with his own style. That same record shows that no major writer was ever more concerned with comparative systems of magic, mysticism and mythology.

What I will examine in this preliminary study is the vital relationship between Yeats's ideas about poetry and his belief in and practice of magic. We have long deprecated Yeats's firm and persistent use of the symbols, rhetoric and methods of what we have termed the 'occult' world. Living in an age in which 'Science, separated from Philosophy, is the opium of the suburbs',[2] we have often failed to understand even the distinction he made between magic and mysticism. Though he initially tended to use the terms interchangeably, he always prefers the words 'Magic', and 'Magician'. Later he saw a subtle but important difference between being a mystic and being a magician: the mystic passively submits to a system while the magician is a creator, a controller of systems. The distinction between mysticism and magic is central to our understanding of Yeats because his idea of a magician is strikingly similar to his idea of a poet; all poets share some of the power of the magician and the greater the poet the more conscious he will be of the links between magic and poetry.

Yeats's earliest statements on mysticism reveal the connections he saw between it and his poetry. He also indicates his desire to use the knowledge he would gain from his researches, and not to be drawn into a cult. In July 1892 he explained to John O'Leary:

> The mystical life is the centre of all that I do and all that I think and all that I write. . . . It bears the same relation to my work as the philosophy of Godwin held to the work of Shelley. . . . I have always considered myself a voice of what I believe to be a greater renascence – the revolt of the soul against the intellect – now beginning in the world.[3]

Though the greater renascence which the young poet saw beginning was more wish than reality, his position is clear and remained much the same throughout his life. Yeats's refusal to submit his ego to any system and his concomitant hatred of passivity are integral to his ever-evolving, eclectic philosophy. In his later life we also see his active eclecticism and his persistent connection between magic and poetry, the magician and the poet.

In 1931 he wrote to Olivia Shakespear asking her the name of 'the Chinese book – golden flowers or whatever it is – . . . .'[4] When the book arrived he thanked her saying, 'the invaluable Chinese book has come. . . . That Chinese book has given me something I have long wanted, a study of meditation that has not come out of the jungle'.[5] The 'Chinese book' is, as Wade suggests, *The Secret of the Golden Flower*, edited by Richard Wilhelm and with a commentary by C. G. Jung.[6] It is a system of Chinese Yoga based on the fundamental concepts of Taoism.

The central activity of the *T'ai I Chin Hua Tsung Chih* as set forth in *The Secret of the Golden Flower* involves a mystic, or meditator, who summons a symbol, or *mandala*, from his own unconscious store and attains unity of being through exclusive contemplation of it. As the commentary in the edition used by Yeats says, 'the method or conscious way by which to unite what is separated, . . . the union of opposites on a higher level of consciousness, . . . [is] but a psychic process of development which expresses itself in symbols'.[7] In parallel, Yeats describes the method of the Chinese system when he writes:

> Day after day I have sat in my chair turning a symbol over in my mind, exploring all its details, defining and again defining its elements, testing my convictions and those of others by its unity, attempting to substitute particulars for an abstraction like that of algebra. I have felt the convictions of a lifetime melt though at an age when the mind should be rigid, and others take their place, and these in turn give way to others. . . . Then I draw my-

self up into the symbol and it seems as if I should know all if I could but banish such memories and find everything in the symbol.[8]

As Yeats used the *mandalas* of the *T'ai I Chin Hua Tsung Chih*, so too he uses the symbols of poetry. For him, the rituals of magic and of poetry are the same: Yeats uses *mandalas* or symbols to unite the conscious and the unconscious within himself and thus to open himself to a whole knowledge.

Yeats's use of *The Secret of the Golden Flower* indicates not only the duration of his association with magical/mystical systems but also the breadth and sophistication of his reading in the area. To have understood the *T'ai I Chin Hua Tsung Chih* required of him a knowledge of the fundamental principles of Chinese thought as expressed in Buddhism and the *I Ching* (with which he was also familiar). Despite his opinion that he was a smatterer, a self-judgement unquestioned by many critics,[9] no poet has a more demonstrably exhaustive background in philosophy, mythologies, religions, magic and mysticism.

He went to the Golden Dawn, to Blavatsky and Mathers, to Blake and to Irish Mythology and Folk-lore for the same purpose that he asked for and read the *Golden Flower* – to learn how to construct a system, which was to make him a great poet. In his description of his childhood and early manhood in *Reveries over Childhood and Youth*, Yeats saw a pattern which he structured into his narrative. The pattern links his experience of what he calls the supernormal to his awareness of himself as a poet. His early associations with Blavatsky and Theosophy and with Mathers and Cabbalism also marked his initial work, especially some of the poetry in *Crossways* (1889). In his diaries, his *Reveries*, his reviews and essays, as well as in his first poetry, Yeats left a record of his early search for a system.

Yeats also turned to Blake in his search, and in the Ellis-Yeats edition and in the two later essays contained in *Essays and Introductions*, he clarifies what he learned from a major English poet who worked from an occult system. But Yeats did not find that his work with Theosophy, Cabbalism and Blake gave him either the system or the subject matter for his own poetry. During the 'nineties he turned to Ireland and politics and attempted to integrate his interests. The attempt led Yeats to what he named *Hodos Chameliontos* and eventually out to his assertion of belief in the *Anima Mundi*.

As he moved into the twentieth century, Yeats made his first public statement of belief in magic in his 1901 essay called 'Magic'. During the period from 1900 to 1914 he made a major effort to change the form of his poetry, turning to drama to learn how to employ the direct and powerful voice he believed necessary for his work. By 1912 Yeats had established a synthesis from Ireland, magic and poetic form which came together in *Ego Dominus Tuus* and enabled him to begin to write his mature and responsible poetry. Yeats's ideas about poetry, especially about its necessary clarity of form, and about magic are so closely associated that to understand one is to understand both in the years of his apprenticeship before *Respcnsibilities*. I believe that our full understanding of the work of one of our greatest poets depends upon our recognition of the place of magic in his development and in his great poetry. I offer this study as a beginning of the exploration of the link between Yeats's magic and his poetry.

NOTES

[1] Dorothy Wellesley, *Letters on Poetry from W. B. Yeats to Dorothy Wellesley* (London: Oxford University Press, 1964), p. 194.
[2] W. B. Yeats, *Explorations* (London: Macmillan, 1962), p. 340.
[3] W. B. Yeats, *Letters to John O'Leary and His Sister*, ed. Allan Wade (New York: Macmillan, 1955), p. 14. Hereafter referred to as *Letters*.
[4] *Letters*, p. 786.
[5] *Letters*, p. 788.
[6] *The Secret of the Golden Flower*, trans. Richard Wilhelm (London: Kegan Paul, Trench, Trubner and Co., Ltd., 1932).
[7] *Ibid.*, pp. 95-96.
[8] W. B. Yeats, *A Vision* (London: Macmillan, 1962), p. 301.
[9] See Richard Ellmann, *Yeats: the Man and the Masks* (London: Faber and Faber, 1949); F. A. C. Wilson, *W. B. Yeats and Tradition* (London: Methuen, 1958).

Acknowledgements

I wish first to thank Professor Joseph Satin of Fresno State University who introduced me to Yeats during a Minnesota Winter fifteen years ago. For his advice, direction and sensitive reading of my manuscript, I owe an immeasurable debt to Professor Donald J. Gray of Indiana University.

I am also indebted to several others who read and commented on my work: Niall Sheridan of Dublin, who graciously read but more graciously shared his memories and his deep understanding of Yeats with me; Professors R. J. Kaufmann, Josephy Malof and Thomas Whitbred of The University of Texas at Austin all made helpful comments. Peter Moscow read and encouraged; he is the kind of reader I hope this book enjoys.

Without the Fellowship granted me by The American Association of University Women, I would not have been able to do the research in Ireland necessary to this book. The AAUW does not bear any responsibility for my statements in this book; nor does anyone but myself.

Without friends like Professor Robert O'Kell, I could never have written this book. Nor could I have done it without Jonathan and Benjamin; I hope that Yeats is for them as he is for us.

Finally, my thanks to Senator Michael B. Yeats, Miss Anne Yeats, to Macmillan Publishers Ltd., London, and The Macmillan Publishing Co. Inc., New York, for their permission to quote extracts from the writing of W. B. Yeats, and Alf MacLochlainn and The National Library of Ireland for all their help.

CHAPTER I

Reveries, Theosophy and Cabbalism: The Early Years

Part I

Throughout his career Yeats devoted much time and energy to the unity of poetry and magic, and it is clear that from the beginning he associates poetry with myth, intuition and the magical world. Writing in 1937, he traces the roots of his subject matter to

> ... something I have received from the generations, part of that compact with my fellow men made in my name before I was born. I cannot break from it without breaking from some part of my own nature, and sometimes it has come to me in supernormal experience; I have met with ancient myths in my dreams, brightly lit; and I think it allied to the wisdom or instinct that guides a migratory bird.[1]

We will never know how often Yeats found the subject for a poem in magical sources such as supernormal experience and dreams, but we know from this statement that he believed all of his subject matter linked to the magical world. Despite the biographies of Hone, Jeffares and Ellmann,[2] we know little about how Yeats arrived at this position, and if we are to understand how magic and poetics function in his poetry, we need to understand more about his life.

Speaking of Lionel Johnson, Yeats said,

> A poet is by the very nature of things a man who lives with entire sincerity, or rather, the better his poetry the more sincere his life. His life is an experiment in living and those that come after have a right to know it. Above all it is necessary that the lyric poet's life should be known, that we should understand that his poetry is no rootless flower but the speech of a man.[3]

Coming to know the experiments of Yeats's life is akin to fitting together pieces of a highly complex jigsaw puzzle. It has been suggested by Hugh Kenner and others that to read any of the *Collected Poems* outside the framework of the total book is to risk partial understanding. More and more it seems likely that this statement may be stretched to apply to Yeats's total *oeuvre*. His *Autobiographies,* for example, should be a primary starting point in our attempts to understand the development of his life and art; instead, it has been criticized as incomplete, vague and more puzzling than illuminating. George Russell's comment on the first volume, *Reveries over Childhood and Youth,* was that Yeats's memories were '. . . the most vacant things a man ever wrote, pure externalities, well written in a dead kind of way, but quite dull except for the odd flashes. The boy in the book might have become a grocer as well as a poet.'[4] The 'odd flashes' Russell noticed may have been more significant than he thought.

Reveries Over Childhood and Youth appeared in 1915, one year after *Responsibilities,* Yeats's first collection which exhibited a consistent change from his early style. *Reveries* was not written as simple autobiography but rather as the beginning of an exorcism of Yeats's past career and a reconstruction of his memories into a coherent shape. As much as *Responsibilities* signals the end of one phase of his poetry and the beginning of another, *Reveries* marks the end of an important period in his life and points, perhaps obliquely, toward the future. Taken as complementary statements, the books illuminate each other and indicate how important magic was in Yeats's life and poetry.[5]

Reveries covers the years up to 1896 revealing a definite pattern in Yeats's memories. He is not so much interested in recounting family tensions as he is in linking what he calls 'supernormal' events with his growing awareness of himself as a poet. Yeats chose his memories deliberately to stress the important and close connection he saw, even in his early years, between magic and the supernormal world and his own poetry.

He begins:

> My first memories are fragmentary and isolated and contemporaneous, as though one remembered some first moments of the Seven Days. It seems as if time had not yet been created, for all thoughts are connected with emotion and place without sequence.[6]

Without humour, Yeats cites his beginning as microcosmic of the beginnings of all creation. But we are told soon after that he remembers 'little of childhood but its pain'.[7] The unhappiness and pain stemmed from 'loneliness' and 'fear', fear of his grandfather,

REVERIES, THEOSOPHY AND CABBALISM: THE EARLY YEARS

William Pollexfen, not of his father as Ellmann would have it.[8] The loneliness of his early days later crystallized into an awareness of alienation[9] which combined with a sense of cosmic importance to mark his life. If any tone characterizes this section of the *Autobiographies* it is that of alienation from others and from himself, of difference in an important, though then uncomprehended way. From the first paragraph of this impressionistic self-history, we confront a man who remembers himself to have been not only remarkable but, at least as strongly, very lonely.

But, if alienation dominates the tone of Yeats's *Reveries*, the sequence of his chosen memories is even more interesting. To sketch lightly what has been well covered elsewhere, he was the eldest son of John Butler Yeats and Susan Pollexfen Yeats. His father was an improvident, moderately successful artist who had been trained for the law. From the little we know, his mother was a quiet woman who preferred exchanging tales with servants to any other activity. In one of the two references made to his mother (the second is a brief account of her paralytic stroke and subsequent death), Yeats says, 'She read no books, but she and the fisherman's wife would tell each other stories that Homer might have told, pleased with any moment of sudden intensity and laughing together over any point of satire'.[10] This remains one of the few comments we have in which the poet suggests a connection between his mother's influence and his art. He was to write later that 'Homer is my example and his unchristened heart',[11] suggesting that he believed some of his most important poetic instincts were inherited from his mother and her family. But it was his father who said of his son, 'By marriage with the Pollexfens I have given a tongue to the sea cliffs of Sligo'.[12]

In view of the importance Yeats and his critics have attributed to his relationship with his father, his lack of analysis of his mother's influence is notable. Ellmann, in *Yeats: The Man and The Masks*, attaches much importance to J. B. Yeats's part in shaping his son's work and, indeed, his psyche. Yeats's rationalistic, highly opinionated father was an instrumental force in his son's life as the record of their letters verifies. And though Yeats rebelled against his father's opinions strongly, it would be misleading to assume that a majority of the poet's interests and achievements resulted from his negative reactions.

Yeats was not perpetually in revolt against his father though he never accepted the Lockean ideals which the elder Yeats espoused. The influences Yeats's mother exerted were often non-verbal, while J. B. Yeats was verbal and persistent to a remarkable degree.

But Yeats clearly saw himself as the descendant of the Pollexfens and the Yeatses. The Pollexfens were important not only for the instinctual inheritance which he valued highly but also for the link to the Anglo-Norman Butlers of whom Yeats was paradoxically proud. But *Reveries* tells us little more about his parents than that Yeats saw them as divergent personalities bound into their separate worlds, not aware of much more than that their son was shy, sensitive and nervous.[13]

He remembers himself as an extremely slow learner, having difficulty learning to read and never doing well in school. He tells us:

> I was unfitted for school work, and though I would often work well for weeks together, I had to give the whole evening to one lesson if I was to know it. My thoughts were a great excitement, but when I tried to do anything with them, it was like trying to pack a balloon into a shed in a high wind. I was always near the bottom of my class, and was always making excuses.[14]

The memory of his apparent slowness seems to have plagued him throughout his life, despite his extensive reading. It has been suggested that given the evidence barring stupidity, Yeats must have been a classic case of late development. I would suggest rather that his preference for solitude[15] and a mind which a neurologist might describe as having too many neurons firing at once (hyper-synapsis) were at the root of his difficulty. What seemed at first a negative aspect of his make-up was in fact an early and continuing source of genius. Yeats apparently recognized something of this himself. Shortly after he published *Reveries*, the metaphor of the balloon provided the base for the quatrain:

> Hands do what you're bid:
> Bring the balloon of the mind
> That bellies and drags in the wind
> Into its narrow shed.[16]

He was never to become a scholar or, as some critics have lamented, an intellectual. His mind could never settle on an exclusive labour for long; even to write a poem was to try to pack a balloon into a 'narrow shed'. So, rather than scholar or intellectual, he became poet, dramatist, essayist, politician, and critical theoretician.

But as Yeats records it in *Reveries*, his early slowness was part of the general blandness of his childhood. The earliest mention of anything which might be connected with his later work is his re-

REVERIES, THEOSOPHY AND CABBALISM: THE EARLY YEARS

counting of a prophetic dream he had as a child. He dreamed that his grandfather was on a steamer which was wrecked and the next morning his grandfather returned home having been shipwrecked.[17] This incident signals the beginning of what I mentioned earlier as a deliberate pattern in *Reveries* for shortly afterwards he makes his first statement about his poetry. The description of his prophetic dream is part of his remembrance of Sligo, and it is there he says that he first hoped to find his audience when he began to write.[18] It is not until he records his earliest memory of the supernormal in his life that Yeats indicates any awareness of himself as a poet. And this is the pattern which recurs in *Reveries* and provides the structure for the volume – memory of supernormal event followed by a statement about poetry.

He again juxtaposes his perception of himself as poet with a memory of supernormal events when he tells us that he wished to make his poetry 'as emotional as possible but with an emotion which [he] described as cold',[19] and then records an event during which he saw strange lights on a hill which he believed to be the sign of the sidhe moving about.[20] As a result of this experience he begins to tell people, '. . . that one should believe whatever had been believed in all countries and periods, and only reject any part of it after much evidence, instead of starting all over afresh and only believing what one could prove'.[21] Here Yeats seems to point to his earliest inclination to believe in what he later called the Great Memory, which was connected in his thinking and his poetry to mythology and magic.

Yeats's pattern of recounting supernormal experiences in close proximity to his statements about poetry is, I think, far from accidental. The same careful structuring evident in his books of poetry exists in this volume as well. But as he wrote *Reveries*, building in the structure of magic and poetry, he was conscious of another element he saw linked to the work he was to do: sexuality. So, in *Reveries*, we find that the first time he conceived of himself as a poet was at the time he became aware of sex. 'The great event of a boy's life is the awakening of sex . . . it all came upon me when I was close upon seventeen like the bursting of a shell', he tells us.[22] He was given to long walks in the country at this time and 'began to play at being a sage, a magician, or a poet'.[23] For Yeats, to be a poet was to be sexually potent and to be a sage and magician too. Sex, magic and poetry were to be part of the same whole for him, and as he presents his early years in this book, he dimly perceived the connection even then.

But Yeats's path toward believing that magic, poetry and sex were connected really started in 1883 when he left school, rejected the family tradition of attendance at Trinity College, and went to art school. There he met AE, George Russell, who was already deeply involved in esoteric reading and painted visions rather than the models before him. Their friendship lasted, through deep disagreements, until Russell's death in 1935. Yeats was predisposed to an interest in Eastern philosophy, having rejected earlier flirtations with science. Russell's reading during this time, to which he probably introduced Yeats, included *The Sacred Books of the East*, edited by Max Müller, *The Buddhist Sutras* (1881), *The Bhagavad-Gita* (1882), and *The Upanishads* (1884). He had also begun reading theosophical literature such as Alfred Percy Sinnett's *Esoteric Buddhism* and Mabel Cook's *Light on the Path*.[24] In Ellmann's words, Russell was a 'godsend' to Yeats; it is probable that he introduced him to the first systematic reading in a field where 'the dream of the magician was no longer an absurdity'.[25] He and Russell were part of a group which formed in 1885 in Dublin to study magic, mysticism and Eastern Religion.[26] Other members of the Dublin Hermetic Society were Charles Weekes, who later wrote mystical poems, Claude Wright, who spent most of his life working for Theosophy, and Yeats's old classmate, Charles Johnston. It met first on 16 June 1885, with Yeats as chairman.[27]

Yeats's address at that meeting exists as an unpublished manuscript, previously quoted by Ellmann. The speech provides some evidence about the state of his thinking on Eastern philosophy at that time in his life. Discussing the purpose of the group, Yeats said:

> Are there observed facts given that all the teachers and the schools of Europe can reduce to no law, facts which they try to reason out of existence as the professors of Genoa sought in the days of the telescope of Galileo to reason the stars out of heaven with the metaphysics of the school men? Yes, there are the observed facts.... But what is all this bother about the immortality of the soul? – it is a great question whether the soul be immortal or not. Has no theology solved that? – no! Fairy tales and legends it has given as these days demand demonstration and experiment – how can it prove anything? Science after science is discovered and shakes mother church that cries let it be anathema. Has not science solved it? Science will tell you the soul of man is a volatile gas capable of solution in glycerine. Take this for your answer if you will, if you will not follow us into the maze of Eastern thought....[28]

Like many young men of his time, Yeats finds science and

REVERIES, THEOSOPHY AND CABBALISM: THE EARLY YEARS

established religion incapable of answering the questions he finds most important – here stated as the nature and immortality of the soul. This may be literally where he started his quest but his search soon widened. Later in 1885, when the Brahmin philosopher Mohini M. Chatterjee visited the Dublin group, Yeats was offered what he later in *Reveries* described as

> ... a philosophy that confirmed my vague speculations and seemed logical and boundless. Consciousness, he [Chatterjee] taught, does not merely spread out its surface but has in vision and contemplation, another motion and can change in height and depth.[29]

Though he took much from Indian philosophy, it is enough to note for the present that what he earlier described as a concern for the 'immortality of the soul' has stretched to include 'consciousness', which he sees as four-fold in direction and collective by implication.

At about the time he began his association with the Dublin Hermetic Society, Yeats met John O'Leary, Fenian and patriarch of the Irish Nationalist Movement. In his *Autobiographies* he credits O'Leary's debates, conversations and freely shared library as the source of 'all I have set my hand to since'.[30] The statement suggests a belief that Irish Nationalism was the well-spring of his poetry, but the matter is more complicated than that. Two ideas had begun to work with equal force on his consciousness: Ireland and Magic. The books O'Leary lent and gave him were not merely political: they convinced Yeats of the special character of the island which he began to see as a microcosm of the world of the spirit, separate from English materialism, the epitome for him of all that was destructive in the Modern World. Though his attitude toward Ireland was anything but static, in his twenties Yeats made of the place what he needed – a special, private retreat, haunted by the vague figures of heroic legend.

The themes of magic, poetry and Ireland which run throughout the volume are stated again in the final sections of *Reveries*. In these final sections, Yeats describes his early experience with psychical research; then he tells us of his first recognition of Ireland as the formal base for the subject matter of his poetry. Finally, he turns again to magic. When he was twenty-one, in 1886, Katherine Tynan took him to a seance.[31] He went in a spirit of characteristic scepticism but during the evening found himself literally possessed:

I was now struggling vainly with this force which compelled me to movements I had not willed, and my movements became so violent that the table was broken. I tried to pray, and because I could not remember a prayer, repeated in a loud voice 'Of Man's first disobedience and the fruit of that forbidden tree whose mortal taste brought death into the world, and all our woe... Sing, Heavenly Muse'.[32]

Yeats often stated his dislike of Milton and his repetition of these lines begs notice. In the winnowing and patterning which accompanied the creation of *Reveries*, he deliberately chose to record the event. By 1886 he had had some poetry published but was uncertain of his poetic career; by 1915 when he published the first section of his autobiography he *was* a poet and had embarked on the second phase of his work where he would explore, as Milton sought to, the roots of 'Man's first disobedience'. But more importantly, Yeats seeks to emphasize his unwillingness to submit his will during the seance. And, what he chose to keep him from submission was, significantly, poetry.

The whole of *Reveries* speaks most of the growing confidence Yeats felt about his role as a poet and often associated with his idea of himself as a poet is a statement of the place magic filled in his development. The pattern he structures into *Reveries* consistently links supernormal experience (prophetic dream, perception of the light of the Sidhe) with his increasing self-awareness as poet. For all of this confidence, the conclusion to the volume strikes a strangely uncertain note:

> For some months now I have lived with my own youth and childhood, not always writing indeed but thinking of it almost every day, and I am sorrowful and disturbed... when I think of all the books I have read, and the wise words I have heard spoken, and of the anxiety I have given to parents and grandparents, and of the hopes I have had, all life weighed in the scales of my own life seems to me a preparation for something that never happens.[33]

In counterpoint to the confidence he earlier stressed, Yeats proposes an antithetic possibility: perhaps his life has been but a preparation for something that never happens. But the antithesis led to poetic creation, for the lines are a paraphrase of what was later to become the prose topic for 'Among School Children': 'Topic for poem – school children and the thought that life will waste them, perhaps that no possible life can fulfill their own dreams or even their teacher's hope. Bring in the old thought that

REVERIES, THEOSOPHY AND CABBALISM: THE EARLY YEARS

life prepares for what never happens'.[34] The note of apology mixed with anxiety that we see here links *Reveries* firmly to *Responsibilities* and less obviously but just as closely to one of Yeats's greatest poems. Yeats wrote in 1914–1915 that his life and his poetry up to that time had been 'a preparation for what never happens'. But juxtaposed with this statement is the rest of the book which expresses the knowledge that he is a poet, the intuition that he is perhaps even a great poet, and suggests in his associations of poetry with his early supernormal experiences and with magic and the myths of Ireland, that the years 1865 to 1886 held the seeds for all that was to come.

Part II

The second section of *Autobiographies* was written between the years 1922 and 1926, when it was published together with *Reveries over Childhood and Youth*. By then Yeats had published eight books of poetry – since *Responsibilities* had come *The Wild Swans at Coole* (1919) and *Michael Robartes and the Dancer* (1921); he was at work on the poems for *The Tower* (1928). As he wrote *Reveries* when he entered a new phase of his poetic career, he wrote *The Trembling of the Veil* as he was about to shift fully into what most critics regard as his most successful and mature style. But it is perhaps more important to notice that Yeats's work on the second section of his autobiography coincides with his writing of the first edition of his most controversial book: *A Vision*, written between 1917 and 1925 and later revised for the 1937 edition. Between 1922 and 1926, then, he worked almost exclusively on *The Trembling of the Veil* and *A Vision*. It might simply be said that the two books clarify each other, or that one *must* read one to understand the other; most accurately, though, one might say that many of the important principles of *A Vision* exist in the second section of *Autobiographies*.

The *Trembling of the Veil* is the last of Yeats's consciously autobiographical attempts (the sections included by Macmillan in the 1955 edition of *Autobiographies* were not intended by Yeats as strictly autobiographical), and it covers only the period of the 'nineties in his life. As he suggests that his childhood and youth held the seeds of all that was to come, he believed that the 'nineties were the years when his beliefs about poetry, politics, history, mythology and magic were consciously formed. He saw himself always as a product of that age and devoted much of his prose to explaining to himself and his audience how he came to survive and break from what he termed, 'the tragic generation'. With everything else, *The Trembling of the Veil* is Yeats's examination of why and how he moved from being a remarkable late Victorian poet to his final position as one of the great modern poets.

His recollections of the 'nineties centre as much on his perceptions of the people around him as they do on himself. He writes in the preface to *The Trembling of the Veil*:

> They were artists and writers and certain among them men of genius, and the life of a man of genius, because of his greater sincerity, is often an experiment that needs analysis and record. At least my generation so valued personality that it thought so.[35]

The artists and writers of whom Yeats speaks are men such as Lionel Johnson, AE (George Russell), Ernest Rhys, Douglas Hyde, Standish O'Grady, Oscar Wilde, William Sharp, John Synge, Ernest Dowson, Edward Dowden, Arthur Symons and Paul Verlaine. Some of these names are now unfamiliar since none attained as high a place in our literature as did Yeats. And yet these were men with whom he shared what he counted as his most important period; he learned from them, shared his work with them, and watched many of them die, ruined, dissipated, reviled.

Though he never attended university, from these people and from others he met through his interest in politics and magic he received a superior education to that which any university since the Middle Ages could have offered. *The Trembling of the Veil* traces his growth from a young man who made 'a new religion, an almost infallible church of poetic tradition',[36] and wished for a world where he could 'discover this tradition perpetually, and not in pictures and in poems only, but in tiles round the chimneypiece and in the hanging that kept out the draught! . . .'[37] to the man who would later see that 'The dream of my early manhood, that a modern nation can return to Unity of Culture, is false. . .'.[38] As we will see, however, Yeats never completely gave up his dream; he learned in the period of the 'nineties that it must be tempered and modified. Yeats's persistence in the belief that poetry was a way to unity of being and of culture differentiated him from the men with whom he shared the 'nineties. Yeats himself recognized this but in *The Trembling of the Veil* he emphasizes again another aspect of his difference: his steady and ever more conscious pre-

REVERIES, THEOSOPHY AND CABBALISM: THE EARLY YEARS

occupation with magic and his consistent association of magic and poetry. Perhaps it was these differences which allowed the poet to escape the ruin around him.

The structure of *The Trembling of the Veil* reinforces the above observations. It resembles musical structure in stating a theme and then amplifying and refining several variations; and the leitmotif is that of magic and poetry. Like *Reveries*, *The Trembling of the Veil* is somewhat skeletal, and only by examining more closely some of Yeats's statements about this period in his life can we fully understand the basis of his career. Thus, I am not working solely from the autobiography in what follows. But, in looking at the first of the five books contained in *The Trembling of the Veil*, 'Four Years: 1887–1891', we see Yeats not only setting up the major themes of the work but preoccupied with two of them: Theosophy and Blake.

In 1889 he published, with John O'Leary's help, *The Wanderings of Oisin*, the long narrative poem he began in 1886; in 1890 'The Lake Isle of Innisfree' was published in *The National Observer*. It was these two poems as much as *Crossways* (1889) which established him as a poet. But Yeats was not satisfied with his work. He remembers:

> For ten or twelve years more I suffered continual remorse. . . . My very remorse helped to spoil my early poetry, giving it an element of sentimentality through my refusal to permit any share of an intellect which I considered impure.[39]

His poverty during this time is legendary. Mostly to earn a few pounds he published editions such as *Irish Fairy and Folk Tales* (1888) and *Representative Irish Tales* (1890), and wrote several review articles. Only the work he did on the fairy and folk tales did he later consider justified. As he looked back at the work he would say that though the pay was bad, he 'did it for his own purposes'.[40] He began to see that he must root his poetry in Irish myth and history. His reconstructed feeling was that

> If Shelley had nailed his Prometheus, or some equal symbol, upon some Welsh or Scottish rock, . . . [his] art would have entered more intimately, more microscopically, as it were, into our thought and given perhaps to modern poetry a breadth and stability like that of ancient poetry.[41]

The events which he regarded as most important during 1887–1891, however, did not concern Irish myth but rather Eastern thought, especially Theosophy, Indian thought and Cabbalism. During these years he met Madame Blavatsky and MacGregor Mathers. With Blavatsky he learned the bases for his lifelong interest in Eastern thought; with Mathers he first conducted successful magical experiments as a member of a Cabbalistic society. Yeats tells us that the reason he was attracted to Theosophy was connected to his rejection of the world represented by Huxley, Tyndall, and Bastian-Lepage. He sought 'sovereignty... over those strong and secret things and thought which others fear and know not'.[42] The statement is over-dramatic. He was hardly alone, then or now, in his dissatisfaction with science and empiricism. His fascination with the figure of the magician probably attracted him to Theosophy as much as any negative reason. Madame Blavatsky was such a figure for him, and though she had recently been discredited by the Society of Psychical Research in London, Yeats went to her in London in 1887 believing that:

> Certainly if wisdom existed anywhere in the world it must be in some lonely mind admitting no duty to us, communing with God only, conceding nothing from fear or favour. Have not all peoples, while bound together in a single mind and taste, believed that such men existed and paid them that honour, ... which they have refused to philanthropists and to men of learning?[43]

He did not so much believe in Blavatsky as he wished himself to become one of the lonely, wise, and courageous minds gifted with knowledge of 'strong and secret things.'

His earlier association with the Dublin Hermetic Society was marked by the visit of Mohini Chatterjee, who represented one of the two major schools of Indian thought: Vedantism. Vedantism stresses that:

> Those who die, insofar as they imagined beauty or justice, are made part of that beauty or justice and move the minds of living men, as Shelley believed; and that mind overshadows mind even among the living and by pathways that lie beyond the senses; and that ... by this measure ... the hermit [is] above all other labourers, because being the most silent and hidden he lived nearer to the Eternal powers, and showed their mastery of the world.[44]

The Brahmin also taught them, 'that all action and words that lead to action were a little vulgar, a little trivial'.[45]

George Russell accepted the Vedantic ideal of asceticism and renunciation represented by Mohini Chatterjee; Yeats did at the time but shortly rejected these aspects of the message. It was Russell's total acquiescence in the mystic ideal which caused many of the quarrels between the two men and finally led Yeats to characterize his friend as a 'Saint Simeon Stylites upon his pillar, Saint Anthony in his cavern, [like] all whose preoccupation is to seem nothing; to hollow their hearts till they are void and without form'.[46] What Yeats took from Vedantism is best seen in his 1928 poem, 'Mohini Chatterjee'.[48]

> I asked if I could pray,
> but the Brahmin said,
> 'Pray for nothing, say
> Every night in bed,
> "I have been a king,
> I have been a slave,
> Nor is there anything,
> Fool, rascal, knave,
> That I have not been,
> And yet upon my breast
> A myriad heads have lain".'[49]

He had earlier encountered the idea of reincarnation in the folk stories and legends of Western Ireland. Here he restates it as Chatterjee told him, but reworked to the point where he controls the ideas and can place them in a concise and assertive form.

When he read Madame Blavatsky's two volume work, *Isis Unveiled*, Yeats found that she was not a Vedantist like Chatterjee but interested in *Puranic* or mythological Hinduism, which he found much more congenial. The book stressed the similarities of all old religions and posited a secret doctrine which had created and sustained them. According to Blavatsky, the original Smaragdine (Emerald) tablet was found on the dead body of Hermes (later explained by Blavatsky to be a gloss-name for a series of mystical commentators). It revealed among other more cryptic messages that 'What is below is like that which is above, and what is above is similar to that which is below. . .'.[50] It also stated that one should

> . . ascend with the greatest sagacity from the earth to heaven, and then descend again to earth, and unite together the power of things inferior and superior; thus you will possess the light of the whole world; and all obscurity will fly away from you.[51]

Though Yeats would later find verification in more respectable sources for the basic ideas offered by Blavatsky, it was in *Isis Unveiled* that he found his first statement of correspondences and a theory concerning the unification of apparent opposites. Importantly, these ideas led not to passive acceptance but to greater clarity of vision, to a higher consciousness.

Blavatsky's second work, *The Secret Doctrine*, gave him a glimpse of what Ellmann calls a 'comprehensive cosmology'.[52] Blavatsky asserted that Hermetism and Hinduism are identical and are the two oldest religious philosophies in the world. The main tenets of Theosophy according to her are that there is a basic though indefinable unity between the individual soul and the Universal Oversoul; there is a universal law of periodicity, of polarity and all is in constant flux, and reflux; and every soul must make the 'obligatory pilgrimage . . . through the Cycle of Incarnation in accordance with Cyclic and Karmic Law'.[53] Yeats had undoubtedly encountered some of these ideas in the reading to which Russell had led him. But here, for the first time, he began to see the possibility of a universal source for man's deepest symbols and traditions. Blavatsky declared that every philosophy in the world had its key in the Hindu sacred books and that pre-Vedic Brahmanism and Buddhism were the twin sources of all religions.[54] Yeats accepted this proposition and went on to find verification of it in the European tradition of mysticism.

As manuscript evidence shows, however, Yeats did not easily accept all of Blavatsky's pronouncements. He had great difficulty in signing the pledges necessary for admittance to the esoteric section of the Theosophical Society. His esoteric journal, begun October, 1889, records that he joined the section in Christmas of 1888 and that 'The pledges gave me no trouble except two – promise to work for Theosophy and promise of obedience to HPB in all Theosophical matters'.[55] He finally decided, 'I myself was to be judge as to what Theosophy is (the term is wide enough) and I consider my work at Blake an wholly adequate keeping of the clause'.[56] He vowed obedience only concerning occult practices and further twisted the language of one part of his pledge from 'we believe in her teachers,' to 'I believe M.B.'s teachers are wholly righteous and learned teachers and I have in them all due confidence as from pupil to teacher'.[57] Yeats refused to believe that Blavatsky's teachers were spirits as she had claimed. Characteristically, he maintained his independence as both poet and pupil; it is not simple scepticism he evidences in the journal entries, but rather the balance and sense of his own identity and purpose which marked him apart from his fellow occultists.

Less than a year after his signing of the pledges, he found himself at odds with HPB over the matter of obedience. Even his construction of the pledge could not make him abide submission to her authority. He writes on 20 December 1889, that he wanted a section begun to study 'Occult research'.[58] He doubted that Blavatsky would accept the proposal because of her aversion to 'Black Magic',[59] but was surprised on 30 December by her aquiescence. Yeats seems to have been the guiding spirit of the small group which tried such experiments as raising the ghost of a burnt flower according to the instructions of a seventeenth-century writer on magic.[60] The attempt was unsuccessful but the instructions for the experiment were certainly one of the first contacts he had with alchemy, a subject which fascinated him for years to come. He was to say later that he engaged in the magical experiments to see if the mind could be 'rid of abstraction'. He also did it to test his own powers as magician. Within a short time it became clear that his objects were not those of the group. He was asked to resign in August of 1890 and he complied, stating that the group put too much value on asceticism and the immediate spread of a dogma. It was not the end of his experience with Hermetism and the philosophies of India.

Shortly before his expulsion/resignation from Blavatsky's group, Yeats had joined what he called a Mystical Celtic Order, The Golden Dawn, whose major figure was MacGregor Mathers. He found that the order shared most of the basic beliefs of the Theosophists but that it stressed Cabbalistic magic. As Ellmann points out, Cabbalism has much in common with neo-platonism and has influenced such figures as Henry More and Pico della Mirandola.[61] Yeats became aware early of the connections between Cabbalism and more orthodox tradition, but this is not what influenced him either to join the order or to stay. He concentrated on learning the symbolic system Mathers offered. He credited Mathers with much: he says, 'Though he did not show me the truth, he did what he professed, and showed me a way to it'.[62]

Yeats's systematic introduction to Cabbalism came from Mathers' *The Kabbala Unveiled*. More importantly, he found in Mathers a guide for his magical experiments.[63] For a time, Mathers seemed the archetypal Magician for whom Yeats sought. He modified this attitude after a time but Mathers remained an important teacher and influence. Yeats tells us

... it was through him mainly that I began certain studies and experiences, that were to convince me that images well up before the mind's eye from a deeper source than conscious or subconscious memory.[64]

Although he never revealed all of the information he gleaned from this source, Yeats does cite the kind of magical experiment he found most powerful and significant. Mathers worked with 'coloured geometrical symbols'[65] on cardboard which he would have his students hold to their foreheads. If the symbol worked, 'the visible world would completely vanish, and that world summoned by the symbol take its place'.[66] One evening Mathers gave Yeats a cardboard symbol which he held to his forehead with his eyes closed. Yeats remembers:

> Sight came slowly, there was not that sudden miracle as if the darkness had been cut with a knife, for that miracle is mostly a woman's privilege, but there rose before me mental images that I could not control: a desert and a black titan raising himself up by his two hands from the middle of a heap of ruins. Mathers explained that I had seen a being of the order of Salamanders because he had shown me their symbol, it would have been sufficient that he imagined it.[67]

This vision was to haunt him for the rest of his life and to provide him with a metaphor for one of his greatest poems, 'The Second Coming'. Yeats strongly implies that the image was not solely the result of the cardboard symbol pressed to his forehead but also a kind of archetypal vision which Mathers might just as well have transmitted telepathically. If we know Yeats we know he believed this image of the desert and the titan which is the core of the later poem came from the *Anima Mundi*.

Yeats continued the experiments Mathers taught him throughout his life, modifying them significantly so that the symbol might be concrete, or a purely mental image, or, most importantly, a word. As I mentioned earlier, Yeats's use of the *T'ai I Chin Hua Tsung Chih* is not especially surprising considering his background. The process taught him by Mathers closely parallels that of ancient Chinese Yoga, and Yeats's admiration for the oriental system must have been based somewhat on the pleasure of finding once again that the core philosophies of the world have universal correspondences.

The Trembling of the Veil contains much material important to our understanding of Yeats's development and I will examine more of its five books in later chapters. 'Four Years: 1887-1891,' the first of its five books makes clear the centrality of Theosophy and Cabbalism to his learning during this period. Though it does not exhibit a clear pattern as does *Reveries*, the book solidly states the theme of the importance of Mathers and Blavatsky in his life. As the last lines of *Reveries* led him to write 'Among School Children' so the method Mathers taught him was to lead to at least one of his other great poems. The image of the titan in the desert called up during his early experiments in Cabbalism was to remain with him for years and eventually to produce 'The Second Coming'.

Though the rituals and practices he learned from Cabbalism and Theosophy continued to affect his life and poetry to the end,[68] Yeats would keep learning and exploring new systems and philosophies. Never after his early poetry was the influence of Indian thought to show so clearly. Especially in the poems written between 1885 and 1890, we can see Yeats's preoccupation with Indian themes and concepts, learned primarily from his association with Theosophy and Cabbalism.

Even before he became deeply involved with Theosophy and Indian philosophy Yeats felt himself in need of an alternative to science and Lockean empiricism. As his father's influence waned and he met George Russell at the Metropolitan Art School, he found company and support for his ideas. The verse published at this time indicates the extent of Yeats's dissatisfaction. In 'The Song of the Happy Shepherd',[69] the first poem in the *Crossways* (1889), Yeats rejects science in favour of dreaming and song:

> There is no truth,
> Saving in thine own heart. Seek, then,
> No learning from the starry men,
> Who follow with the optic glass
> The whirling ways of stars that pass;
> Seek then, for this is also sooth,
> No word of theirs: the cold star-bane
> Has torn and rent their hearts in twain,
> And dead is all their human truth.[70]

The Happy Shepherd, in his address to the 'sick children of the world' (l. 6), echoes the attitude of the young Yeats, who felt that dependence on science had destroyed the spiritual and moral values of the old world. The shepherd's celebration of the artist ('Words alone are certain good', l. 10) and his conviction that subjective truth alone is valid similarly mirrors the aesthetic ideas of Yeats and his contemporaries.

But The Happy Shepherd, though clear in his rejection of science and its 'grey truth', is vague in the alternatives he offers:

> Go gather by the humming sea
> Some twisted, echo-harbouring shell,
> And to its lips thy story tell,
> And they thy comforters will be,
> Rewording in melodious guile
> Thy fretful words a little while,
> Till they shall singing fade in ruth:
> For ruth and joy have brotherhood,
> And words alone are certain good –
> Sing, then for this is also sooth.
>
> (2. 14–23)

Yeats has rejected, in this poem, conventional nineteenth-century Western (or perhaps more specifically for him English) values, but he has not yet turned to the East to replace them. His poem is more romantic than Oriental,[71] more a denial of certain ideas than a positive assertion of belief.

The implications of this negative impulse are fully realized in its companion poem, 'The Sad Shepherd'.[72] The Sad Shepherd, following the advice of The Happy Shepherd, romantically seeks solace from nature. Yet he finds himself incapable of communicating his 'piteous story' (1. 9) to star, sea, or dewdrop; and The Happy Shepherd's pearly sea-shell changes the Sad Shepherd's song to 'inarticulate moan' (1. 27). The poem suggests Yeats's awareness of the dangers of extreme subjectivity, refuting the Happy Shepherd's claim that 'words alone are certain good'. The poems reflect the awareness of his need for a philosophy and for a subject matter which reflected more than lonely complaint.

Most of his very early poems were written before 1886, the year in which Yeats met Mohini Chatterjee. Whatever he was later to reconsider, the encounter with Chatterjee gave Yeats's poetry a new impetus, and channelled his vague and mystical longings into specific Indian philosophical ideas. Vedantism, which Chatterjee taught, is dominated by asceticism, stressing that abstract perfection consists in reaching an absolute spiritual stasis achieved by total acceptance and renunciation. Yeats incorporated such a doctrine into two of his explicitly Indian poems, 'An Indian Song' and 'Kanva on Himself,' and also into two verses of 'Quatrains and Aphorisms': [73]

III
Long thou for nothing, neither sad nor gay;
Long thou for nothing, neither night nor day;
Not even 'I long to see thy longing over,'
To the ever-longing and mournful spirit say.

IV
The ghosts went by me with their lips apart
From death's late languor as these lines I read
On Brahma's gateway, 'they within have fed
The soul upon the ashes of the heart.'

'An Indian Song' and 'Kanva on Himself' are Yeats's first poems explicitly Indian in both matter and philosophy; in them he first indicates his acceptance of Chatterjee's Vedantic idealism. The Indian narrator in 'An Indian Song'[74] sings to his love of an island populated by parrots and peacocks where 'great boughs drop tranquillity' (1. 2). On the island far from the 'unquiet lands' (2. 10) he and his love will be 'alone of mortals' (3. 11), so that their love may grow and even in death their 'shades will rove. . / With vapoury footsole by the water's drowsy blaze' (4. 18–20). Only by escaping 'earth's feverish lands' (2. 10) may the Indian and his love find peace. 'Kanva on Himself'[75] is a vision by an Indian seer of his myriad 'other lives' (3. 12). Having been slaves, rajah, lovers and beloveds, 'beyond number' (2. 6), Kanva does not fear 'the usury of Time,/Or Death' (5. 17-18). 'Kanva' later became 'Mohini Chatterjee' and Yeats suppressed the earlier version. The idea of reincarnation, central to both poems as it is to *A Vision*, was never rejected by Yeats. 'Kanva' was suppressed not because of its ideas but rather because of its last stanza which affirms with Chatterjee that the body is 'but garnered rust/Of ancient passions and of ancient fears' (4. 15-16) and that 'as things were so shall things ever be' (5. 20). By the time he rewrote the poem, Yeats accepted neither the renunciation nor the quiet acceptance of fate central to Vedantism. 'Mohini Chatterjee' denies the passivity at the core of 'Kanva' and goes on to describe the power and vitality of reincarnation.

But in his early poetry we often see Yeats recommend solitude and renunciation. In 'The Island of Statues'[76] love can only be achieved at the price of death. Thus, two expendable lovers die for Naschina that she and Antonio may pluck a magic 'scarlet bloom' (III. 196) guarded by an enchantress on a timeless island. All who have previously sought the flower – which will guarantee permanent love – have been turned to stone. Because of the deaths of Colin and

Thernot, Naschina gains the flower, frees Antonio and the other statues and banishes the enchantress. Antonio and Naschina will be king and queen on the island cut off from the world for eternity. Though the subject matter has a vaguely classical cast, the play is shot through with the quietism characteristic of orthodox Vedanta. Yeats transferred Indian themes to Irish subjects in several of his 'island' poems. In 'To an Isle in the Water',[77] for example, the lover wishes to retreat from the disorder of the world to an island of quietness and idleness; and in his 'The Stolen Child',[78] faeries lure a human child to an island free of the 'world's . . . weeping' (1. 12) and 'unquiet dreams' (3. 34).

Yeats himself recognized the escapism which underlay these early poems, and wrote to Katharine Tynan that his 'island' verses were 'almost all a flight into fairyland, and a summons to that fight'. They were not, he added, the poetry of 'insight and knowledge, but of longing and complaint'.[79] Temporarily the asceticism and self-renunciation of Vedanta had fused with Yeats's own poetic imagination. Thus, he could blend Irish subjects with Indian ideas, as in the sonnet 'She Who Dwelt Among the Sycamores',[80] in which quietism is personified in the last two lines:

> 'I am lone Lady Quietness, my sweet,
> And on the loom I weave thy destiny'. (2. 13–14)

Yeats confessed that this poem reflected his own desire to 'rest and to get away from the noise and rumours of the world'.[81] Later, when such quietism no longer attracted him, and when he had rejected Vedantism for the Vedic and Puranic Hinduism taught by Blavatsky, he admitted that he regretted 'that Sycamore poem', and added, 'I think it perfectly detestable and always did'.[82]

At the point when Yeats became dissatisfied with the Vedantism of Chatterjee, he met Madame Blavatsky in London, and in that year 'Jealousy'[83] was written. Like the hero of the poem, Vijaya, who is torn between the love of Anashuya, a worldly priestess, and Amrita, a spiritual figure who bears his mother's name, Yeats was aware of the split within himself between the active philosophy of Blavatsky and the quietism he had so recently embraced. Yeats's note to the *Poems* (1895)[84] states that he meant the poem to be the 'first scene of a play about a man loved by two women, who had one soul between them, one woman waking when the other slept, and knowing but daylight as the other only night'. In 'Jealousy' Vijaya chooses Anashuya as Yeats chose a more active philosophy. By the time he met Blavatsky he had rejected the excessive passiveness of his earlier philosophy in favour of a more dynamic and active one, but as he foresaw, this choice was but the first scene of a more complicated dialectic.

While this shift in philosophy was taking place, Yeats wrote of his awareness of a sense of change in a letter to Katharine Tynan in 1888. He says of his poetry of the previous year:

> I was then living a quiet harmonious poetic life. Never thinking out of my depth. Always harmonious, narrow, calm. . . . Everything done then was quite passionless.[85]

He continues, speaking of his current poetry: 'I have been going about on shoreless seas. Nothing anywhere has clear outline. Everthing is cloud and foam'. Much later he wrote of the change in his use of Indian ideas, saying he now used them

> with the object of trying to lay hands upon some dynamic and substantialising force as distinguished from the eastern quiescent and supersensualizing state of the soul – a movement downwards upon life, not upwards out of life.[86]

This attempt, under the influence of Madame Blavatsky, supported by his reading of Müller's publications of the sacred Hindu texts,[87] led him to an interest in the occult and in supernatural power which begins to reflect in his poetry.

Yeats connects this interest in the occult and in supernatural power specifically with India in 'The Seeker',[88] in which the central figure is an Old Knight who has spent most of his life by 'Asian Rivers' (I. 20) in 'dream-led wandering' (I. 16). He sought a 'visionary one' (II. 71) and has given up his days 'Untouched by human joy or human love' (II. 65); in the end he dies, seeing only the face of 'a bearded witch' (II. 72). To give up life in the search for a visionary ideal, Yeats tells us again, is to die disappointed in an ironic way in 'The Seeker'. Yeats transferred this enchantment and superhuman power to an Irish subject in the 'Fairy Doctor',[89] who professed to know 'by signs of secret wit/The man whose hour of death draws nigh' (2. 5–6) and to be able to cure illnesses with 'many a herb and many a spell' (5. 17). The Celtic magic of the fairy doctor's wisdom corresponds to Yeats's own interest in magic. Such correspondence is more elaborately worked out in 'Time and the Witch Vivien',[90] where Vivien's 'power in spells and secret rites' (1. 6) eventually contributes to her death at the hands of the old pedlar Time. Actually, the poem indicates an undeveloped but important refinement in Yeats's conception of the powers and limitations of magic. Vivien, a witch herself, confuses the pedlar Time with some 'fierce magician' (1. 9), and with Merlin. She attributes her death not only to Time but also to Chance (1. 69). The poem signals Yeats's movement toward a belief that Time and Chance are involved intricately with magic.

With forty-nine years of his best work before him, Yeats had passed through a period in his personal life and in his poetry of intimate involvement with Indian ideas. Though his interest persisted, by 1890 he had thoroughly rejected the Vedantic ideal of self-renunciation that he had come to know through George Russell and Mohini Chatterjee. From now on, his interests would broaden and attain complexity as he began to see the correspondences between Indian philosophies and all others. He would move more and more toward his primary interest in magic, power and poetry. Perhaps this is why Mathers is given relatively more attention in the *Autobiographies* than Blavatsky. But, in his early poetry, both in his 'Indian' poems and in his Irish and lyrical verses, we can see Yeats's developing use of Indian ideas. Indian thought via Theosophy and Cabbalism as well as his earliest experiences in the West of Ireland, as we can see in his pros' and his early poetry, were cornerstones upon which Yeats founded his philosophic and poetic career.

NOTES

[1] W. B. Yeats, *Essays and Introductions* (London: Macmillan, 1961), p. viii.

[2] See Joseph Hone, *W. B. Yeats* (London: Macmillan, 1962); A. Norman Jeffares, *W. B. Yeats, Man and Poet* (London: Routledge and Kegan Paul, Ltd., 1962); and Richard Ellmann, *Yeats: The Man and The Masks* (London: Faber and Faber, 1949).

[3] Quoted from an unpublished speech of W. B. Yeats in Richard Ellmann, *Yeats: The Man and The Masks*, p. 5. Hereafter referred to as *Man and Masks*.

[4] John Eglington, *A Memoir of AE, George William Russell* (London: Macmillan, 1937), p. 111.

[5] The second volume of *Autobiographies*, *The Trembling of the Veil*, appeared in 1926, one year after the first edition of *A Vision*, which, like *Responsibilities*, marked a significant re-evaluation point in Yeats's life. I will discuss *The Trembling of the Veil* later.

REVERIES, THEOSOPHY AND CABBALISM: THE EARLY YEARS

[6] W. B. Yeats, *Autobiographies* (London: Macmillan, 1966), p. 5. Hereafter referred to as *Autobiographies*. If one were to describe the form of the introduction to Joyce's autobiographical *Portrait of the Artist as a Young Man*, it would follow the same pattern as Yeats's introduction to *Reveries*.

[7] *Autobiographies*, p. 11.

[8] *Ibid.*, p. 6.

[9] *Ibid.*, p. 35.

[10] *Ibid.*, p. 61.

[11] W. B. Yeats, 'Vacillation' first printed in eight stanza form in *Collected Poems* (London: Macmillan, 1950); appears in the definitive edition (1956), pp. 245-247.

[12] Joseph Hone, *W. B. Yeats* (London: Macmillan, 1962), p. 17.

[13] *Ibid.*

[14] *Autobiographies*, p. 41.

[15] In 1887 Yeats wrote: 'I like being by myself greatly. Solitude, having no tongue in her head, is never a bore. She never demands of us sympathies we have not; she never makes near war on the distant'. In *The Letters of W. B. Yeats*, ed. Allan Wade (London: Hart-Davis, 1955), p. 34. Hereafter referred to as *Letters*. Despite this early statement, Yeats made himself the centre of one of the largest and most varied circles of friends in his age.

[16] W. B. Yeats, 'The Balloon of the Mind' first printed in *The New Statesman*, September 29, 1917; reprinted in *The Wild Swans at Coole* (Dundrum: Cuala Press, 1917); appears in the definitive edition (1956), p. 153.

[17] *Autobiographies*, pp. 12-13.

[18] *Ibid.*, p. 18.

[19] *Ibid.*, p. 74.

[20] *Ibid.*, pp. 76-77.

[21] *Ibid.*, p. 78.

[22] *Autobiographies*, p. 62.

[23] *Ibid.*, p. 64.

[24] See T. S. Dume, *W. B. Yeats: A Study of His Readings* (Philadelphia: University of Pennsylvania Press, 1950), pp. 23 ff.

[25] *Man and Masks*, p. 42.

[26] See Naresh Guha, *W. B. Yeats: An Indian Approach* (Calcutta: Jadaupur Press, 1968). I am most indebted to Guha for providing me much information on Yeats's Indian interests and for direction in my reading on the subject.

[27] *Man and Masks*, p. 42.

[28] *Ibid.*, p. 43.

[29] *Autobiographies*, p. 92.

[30] *Ibid.*, p. 101.

[31] Virginia Moore, *The Unicorn* (New York: Macmillan, 1954), p. 21.

[32] *Autobiographies*, p. 104.

[33] *Ibid.*, p. 106.

[34] National Library of Ireland MS. 13, 576. Also quoted by Thomas Parkinson, in *W. B. Yeats: The Later Poetry* (Berkeley: University of California Press, 1964), p. 93.

[35] *Autobiographies*, p. 109.

[36] *Ibid.*, pp. 115-116.

[37] *Ibid.*, p. 116.

[38] *Ibid.*, p. 295.

[39] *Ibid.*, p. 188.

[40] *Ibid.*, p. 149.

⁴¹ *Ibid.*, p. 150. Like many of Yeats's statements, this one is interesting in several ways: (a) the rock Shelley should have nailed Prometheus to could not have been English: Yeats always prefers Celtic to British; (b) he is giving us a definition not only of ancient poetry but of modern poetry as well (ancient poetry works because it enters 'intimately . . . microscopically' into our thought; if modern poetry will work it must do the same).
⁴² *Autobiographies*, p. 149.
⁴³ *Ibid.*, p. 173.
⁴⁴ W. B. Yeats, 'The Pathway', in *Collected Works* (London: Macmillan, 1908), VIII, 197. For a fuller discussion of Mohini Chatterji, see Guha.
⁴⁵ *Ibid.*
⁴⁶ *Autobiographies*, p. 247.
⁴⁷ *Ibid.*, p. 246.
⁴⁸ First printed in *The London Mercury*, November, 1930; reprinted in *The Winding Stair and Other Poems* (London: Macmillan, 1933); appears in the definitive edition (1956), pp. 242-243.
⁴⁹ For an instructive analysis of the composition of the poem see Parkinson's *The Later Poetry*, p. 204 ff.
⁵⁰ H. P. Blavatsky, *Isis Unveiled* (California: Theosophy Co., 1925), I, 507.
⁵¹ *Ibid.*
⁵² *Man and Masks*, p. 60.
⁵³ H. P. Blavatsky, *The Secret Doctrine* (Point Loma, California: Theosophical Publishing Co., 1946), p. 17. For a fuller discussion see Alfred Boyd Kuhn, *Theosophy, A Modern Revival of Ancient Wisdom* (New York: Theosophical Press, 1930); and Ellmann's *Man and Masks*.
⁵⁴ *Isis Unveiled*, p. 639. See also Guha, p. 48.
⁵⁵ National Library of Ireland MS. 13, 569.
⁵⁶ *Ibid.*
⁵⁷ *Ibid.*
⁵⁸ *Ibid.*
⁵⁹ *Ibid.*
⁶⁰ *Autobiographies*, p. 181.
⁶¹ *Man and Masks*, p. 90.
⁶² *Autobiographies*, p. 576.
⁶³ *Ibid.*, p. 184.
⁶⁴ *Ibid.*, p. 183.
⁶⁵ *Autobiographies*, p. 185.
⁶⁶ *Ibid.*, p. 186.
⁶⁷ *Ibid.*, pp. 185-86. Yeats is, of course, recalling the experience at a distance of 36-37 years and the reference to 'woman's privilege' is connected more to his later theories on sexuality than to the specific instance he remembers.
⁶⁸ No one is certain of when Yeats dropped out of active membership in the Stella Matutina group which followed Mathers's Golden Dawn. Moore points out that Yeats surely did not belong to a society after 1919 (*Unicorn*, p. 177), but I feel sure that she is in error. He does not mention membership in any society after this time and in 1922 stated that he was not a member of any Cabbalistic Society (*Autobiographies*, p. 575). But it seems likely that he continued membership in the societies for years to come. See George Harper's *Yeats's Golden Dawn* (New York: Macmillan, 1974) which confirms my speculation.

REVERIES, THEOSOPHY AND CABBALISM: THE EARLY YEARS

[69] First published as 'An Epilogue to "The Island of Statues" and "The Seeker"', *Dublin University Review*, October, 1885; reprinted as 'Song of the Last Arcadian' in *Wanderings* (1889); appears in the definitive edition (1956), pp. 7-8.

[70] Most of the 'Crossways' poems in the definitive edition (1956) are considerably different from those which appeared in Yeats's first book of poetry, *The Wanderings of Oisin and Other Poems* (1889); moreover, many of the poems in *Wanderings* have been changed from their original versions in various Irish and English periodicals. For the purposes of this discussion, in which Yeats's changing attitudes towards Indian ideas are considered, all quotations come from the earliest published text. For the textual history of his poems, see *The Variorum Edition of the Poems of W. B. Yeats*, eds. Peter Allt and Russell K. Alspach (New York: Macmillan, 1957).

[71] 'The Song of the Happy Shepherd' does, however, use one idea which may be of Indian origin. Lines 18-19 ('The very world itself may be/Only a sudden flaming word').

[72] First printed as 'Miserrimus' in the *Dublin University Review*, October, 1886; appears in the definitive edition (1956), pp. 8-9.

[73] These verses were first printed in *Wanderings* (1889); never reprinted. See also Guha.

[74] First printed in the *Dublin University Review*, December, 1886, under the title 'An Indian Song'; appears in the definitive edition (1956), p. 14. See also Guha.

[75] First printed in *Wanderings* (1889); never thereafter reprinted.

[76] The entire play was first published in the *Dublin University Review*, April-July, 1885, and thereafter never fully reprinted; appears in the definitive edition (1956), pp. 9-10.

[77] First printed in *Wanderings* (1889); reprinted, with no significant changes, in the definitive edition (1956), p. 20.

[78] First printed in *The Irish Monthly*, December, 1886; appears in the definitive edition (1956), pp. 18-19.

[79] *Letters*, p. 63.

[80] First printed in *The Irish Monthly*, September, 1887; reprinted in *Wanderings* (1889); never thereafter reprinted.

[81] *Letters*, p. 110.

[82] *Letters*, p. 390.

[83] According to Ellmann, *Identity*, p. 287.

[84] W. B. Yeats, *The Variorum Edition of the Poems*, ed., Peter Allt and Russell K. Alspach (New York: Macmillan, 1957), p. 841.

[85] *Letters*, p. 88.

[86] *Letters*, p. 469.

[87] The basic content of the sacred Hindu scriptures, and indeed of Indian philosophy in general which is pertinent to my remarks can be found in Heinrich Zimmer, *Philosophies of India* (New York: Macmillan, 1951).

[88] First published in the *Dublin University Review*, September, 1885; reprinted in *Wanderings* (1889); never thereafter reprinted.

[89] First printed in *The Irish Fireside*, 10 September, 1887; reprinted in *Wanderings* (1889); never thereafter reprinted.

[90] First printed in *Wanderings* (1889); never reprinted.

CHAPTER II

Yeats and Blake: The Beginnings of Confidence and of a System

If two of the cornerstones on which Yeats founded his career were Indian philosophy via Theosophy and Cabbalism, another was surely his reading of William Blake. Yeats's *Autobiographies* provides less information on this topic than could give us a full understanding of the relationship between the two poets. 'The Necessity of symbolism', contained in the Quaritch edition of Blake done by Yeats and Ellis, and Yeats's two later essays, 'William Blake and the Imagination,' and 'William Blake and His Illustrations to *The Divine Comedy*', provide significant information about what Yeats learned from Blake. Primarily, Yeats was engaged in the same attempt in his work with Blake as he had been in his work with Theosophy and Cabbalism: to identify poetry with magic, and as importantly, to learn how to use the knowledge gained from the magical world as a base for his own work. In its broad lines, Yeats's going to Blake follows the same pattern as when he went to Blavatsky and Mathers: he went to them for a system, for confidence, for a language. And Yeats came out the same way from each experience: reluctant to join a system, stubborn in his attempts to use what he learned, and determined to put his knowledge together in a way that was his own.

Most of Yeats's critics have acknowledged a link between him and Blake, but the link turns quickly to a comparison, and in the comparison Yeats often loses. In his important study, *Blake and Yeats: The Contrary Vision*, Hazard Adams set the angle from which critics would view the relation between the two poets for years. He states that:

> The book is not primarily about Blake's influence upon Yeats.... My attitude toward the question of Blake's influence upon Yeats is, first, that it is not the most important question in a comparison of the two poets and, second, that in many cases

Blake's influence can never be sorted out from the influences which played upon both Blake and Yeats.[1]

Adams is vague both in his prefatory statement and throughout the book about what the influences which played upon both poets were; though clearly the most significant common influence on both was that of occult studies. He draws an almost imperceptible line between influence and comparison, faulting Yeats first for misreading Blake and then for not being properly influenced.

In the recent major commentary on Yeats and Blake, Bloom's chapter, 'Blake and Yeats', in *Yeats*,[2] we find most of Adams's prejudices upheld and significant new ones added. Yeats's reading of Blake, undertaken for an edition with Edwin Ellis, never had a chance of success because 'The mid-century Blake revival . . . had left the text of Blake in dreadful condition, a condition that Ellis and Yeats worsened unbelievably'. The edition, Bloom says,

> is a monument to the arrogance and ignorance of Ellis, and to Yeats's second great struggle with the Covering Cherub of Poetic Influence, a struggle productive in this edition of some gorgeous nonsense, and much more plain nonsense, and productive also, decades later, of *A Vision* and many of its allied poems and plays.

Unlike previous apologists who have cited everything from nervous fatique to poor eyesight to explain Yeats's work on the edition, Bloom simply dismisses Yeats's reading as 'gorgeous' and 'plain' nonsense.[3] But more importantly, Bloom dismisses Yeats's understanding of Blake as a struggle with 'the Covering Cherub of Poetic Influence.' This concept is central to Bloom's argument not only about Yeats and Blake, but about all of Yeats's work. In misreading Blake, 'Yeats performs the true work of the poet, and is found by his *clinamen,* his own movement out and away from Blake'.[4] Blake was Yeats's covering cherub, or shadow, as Milton was for Blake. To escape the cherub Yeats had to misread:

> Yeats's misunderstanding is so fundamental that it scarcely can be misunderstanding, but must be deliberate, an example of that *clinamen* or creative swerve away from the precursor. . . .[4a]

Too much of the concept of *clinamen* speaks of poetry as the result of neurosis. Yeats's understanding of Blake is far too important to reduce to pseudo-Freudian analysis.

Bloom and Adams measure Yeats by Blake and find him wanting. Their critiques fail to look at Yeats as *another*, and *different* poet who studied Blake at an early point in his development and learned much from him. To attempt to trace influence directly from one poet to the other, I would agree with Bloom and Adams, is unproductive. But comparison of Blake and Yeats seems to me equally fruitless. The real problems which still exist in any discussion of Yeats and Blake are first, why Yeats chose to study him (though he did much editing almost solely for money, the small pay for this project could hardly have been its attraction); and second, what exactly he took from his study.

Yeats was first introduced to Blake by his father when he was 'fifteen or sixteen,'[5] then reading him in the light of pre-Raphaelitism. Later, in 1889, he and Edwin Ellis, a friend of Yeats's father, agreed to collaborate on an edition of Blake's works. He wrote to Katharine Tynan in February of 1889:

> You will be surprised to hear that I am at besides the new play [The Countess Cathleen]; a commentary on the mystical writing of Blake. A friend is helping me as he knows Blake much better than I do, or anyone else perhaps. It should draw notice . . . for there is no clue printed anywhere to the mysterious 'Prophetic Books' – Swinburne and Gilchrist found them unintelligible.[6]

Ellis and Yeats worked on the three volume edition and commentary, published by Bernard Quaritch, for four years. Blake was important to Yeats's imagination to some extent for the rest of his life; it is still possible, however, to overrate Blake's influence on his student. The accuracy of the Ellis-Yeats study has been adequately challenged. By now we may believe it is speculative, sloppy, and of minimal importance to a study of Blake.

But though the Ellis-Yeats edition of Blake is not an ultimately valuable piece of scholarship, it cannot be denied that they were the first to publish *Vala* and *The Four Zoas*. Nor can it be denied that Yeats is the earliest critic of Blake to share with him a background in Cabbalism. Essentially, the best reason for preserving the edition is for what it tells us of Yeats, especially in volume one, *The System*, which is the only volume showing much evidence of his work. What we will see is that Blake did not so much influence Yeats as serve to give him confidence that a major poet could work from an occult system. Yeats did not find a system in Blake but rather confirmed ideas he was adopting from Theosophy and Cabbalism. And when Yeats moves away from Blake in his interpretation of Blake's work, it will always be toward what he had learned from Blavatsky and Mathers.

What Yeats wrote, especially in the preface to volume one and in his essay, 'The Necessity of Symbolism', is clear. He may be misunderstanding Blake to some extent but is also wending his way, albeit tortuously, to his own system, to his subject matter which will be indivisibly welded to his poetic theory. Yeats tells us, 'Here was a myth as well worth study as any that had been offered to the world, since first men learned that myths were briefer and more beautiful than exposition, as well as deeper and more companionable. . . .'[8] He marvels at the 'solidity of the myth . . . and its wonderful coherence'.[9] To the young man who would soon be in the midst of what he called '*Hodos Chameliontos*', bewildered by the confusion of images learned from several sources,[10] aware of the disrepute of the whole area of magic and myth which interested him most, Blake was a saving example and even a discipline. Yeats assures himself and his readers that 'Blake was no mere freak of an eccentric mind but an eddy of that floodtide of symbolism which attained its tide-mark in the magic of the middle ages'.[11] Yeats here identifies magic and myth with poetry, and equally importantly has verified for himself that if Blake's myth grew from Cabbalism and Medieval alchemy and was not a 'freak of an eccentric mind', then he too could work from these sources. Basically, though, Yeats has made the identification, vital to his own work, between poetry and Medieval magic.

Yeats's sense of identification with Blake was not based exclusively on what he recognized as parallel interests. Yeats had begun to move away from the submissive Eastern philosophies represented by both Blavatsky and Chatterjee; he was never to be a worshipper at the shrine of Eastern thought, though he would maintain his interest in the East all of his life. Yeats wanted to be a Western poet/magician, not an Orientalist; he wanted to use the knowledge he was gaining from Theosophy and Cabbalism, and not be used as a simple follower. Blake offered Yeats the example of a Western poet who used the same sources Yeats himself wanted to use and yet created a Western myth not an Eastern one. He began to believe that there were many paths to follow in seeking the truth – all of them connected to magic:

> The Hindu, in the sculptured caverns of Elephanta; the gipsy, in the marking of the sea shell he carries to bring him good fortune; the Rosicrucian student, in the geometric symbols of medieval magic, the true reader of Blake in the entangled histories of Urizen and his children, alike discover a profound answer to the riddle of the world.[12]

Yeats began to see that the paths he was taking were not unique, but ancient and universal: Cabbalists, Hindus, gipsys, true readers of Blake all seek to discover the answer to the riddle of the world. Once again, Yeats has identified magic and poetry. But here he has further identified the magic and poetry as part of a long and universal tradition. He was beginning to understand that his turn to Theosophy, Indian philosophy and Cabbalism was more than a reaction against the rationalism of his father and his age. Yeats's interest in magic and poetry was part of a tradition, the same tradition to which William Blake belonged. Though he was to say as late as 1930 that to recount his magical and spiritualistic experiences was to make himself 'a post for dogs and journalists to defile',[13] each time he repeated the phrase it became more of a pose and less of a certainty; his study of Blake was the beginning of a new confidence within Yeats.

Should we doubt that Yeats saw much of himself in Blake at the time he worked on the edition, we have the evidence of his still unverified claim that Blake was an Irishman, descended from an O'Neill family.[14] Yeats much later admitted Blake to be English. In 1936 he wrote to Ethel Mannin, 'Of course I don't hate the people of England, considering all I owe to Shakespeare, Blake, Morris. . . .'[15] But for a time, the myth of Blake's Irish descent was psychically useful to him. Besides finding support for himself in Blake's interest in magic and in his nationality, Yeats saw other correspondences between their lives. Blake, he tells us, was considered odd by his schoolmates. Then, remembering his own experience, rationalizes for both of them that 'The man or boy of genius is very generally hated or scorned by the average man or boy until the day comes for him to charm them into unwilling homage'.[16] Yeats's perception, based as it is on personal alienation, assumes an interesting twist. It is not merely that he and Blake have been scorned as misunderstood geniuses; they will (like magicians) 'charm' those who have scorned them 'into unwilling homage'. In recounting Blake's life, which Yeats perceived as so like his own, he eerily presages events which were to happen later in his own experience. Of Blake's love for Polly Woods (unfulfilled, as Yeats's love for Maud Gonne was to be) and subsequent marriage to Catherine Boucher, Yeats writes:

> Humiliated by his ill-starred love, he was grateful for a little womanly kindness; and from such gratitude, not for the first time upon the earth, sprang a love that lasted until life had passed away.[17]

Much of Yeats's identification is youthful and romantic; but it served him well and indicates a kind of self-understanding about both his life and his poetry.

Yeats looked upon Blake as a 'teacher before all things';[18] and considered that the whole of his teaching 'could be summed up in a few words'.[19] Yeats's generalization is obviously invalid, but what he wished to see as the essence of Blake is both interesting and nearly accurate. We get a glimpse of Yeats's thinking on the matter of the essence of Blake in the introduction to the Ellis-Yeats edition: 'The foundation of Blake's symbolic system of speech is the conception of the four-fold in Man'.[20] Later, in the second volume, *The Meaning,* we are told (probably by Yeats) that the 'Symbolical Structure of the Mystical Writings . . . is based on a four-fold division: Head, Heart, Loins, Womb. . . .'[21] It is then remarked that this four-fold division is often in triads repeated four times. We are given this example:

South	West	North	East
Head	Loins	Womb	Heart
Africa	America	Europe	Asia

This is very like the late symbolism, pointed out previously by Adams and others, used by Yeats in a letter to Olivia Shakespear describing his 'four quarters' on which he based his system in *A Vision.* The scheme closely resembles part of the rituals Yeats began writing for an Irish Mystical Order while he worked on Blake.

By 1934 he wrote to Olivia Shakespear, saying:

Notice this symbolism

Waters under the earth The Earth	The Bowels etc.	Instinct
The Water	= The Blood and the sex organ	Passion
The Air	= The lungs, logical thought	Thought
The Fire	=	Soul[22]

Yeats had firmly developed the principle of quaternity as the base of his conception of the universe, history, and most importantly, the individual soul. This was at a much later time, far from when he first perceived the four-fold structure in Blake that was to become his own. But an incomplete unpublished manuscript written at the same time he was working on Blake shows that he was already beginning to use this structure for his own purposes as he worked out the initiation rite for the Irish Mystical Order. The rite was to be based on the four ancient Talismans of Ireland: The Sword, The Stone, The Spear, and The Cauldron. Yeats associates each of them with parts of the body, states of the soul, colours, and geographical directions.[23] The notes are extremely detailed, and indicate a clear attempt to link all that he knows about magical structures to Irish mythology and ritual. In an unpublished diary of the same year (1889) he carries on the listing of four-fold divisions describing the four elementary states –

    Heat + Dryness = Fire
    Heat + Moisture = Air
    Cold + Moisture = Water
    Cold + Dryness = Earth

– and also the twelve Zodiacal signs, which he works out in triplicates (for example: Cancer – Crab – ♋).[24] The diary is full of such patterns of fours; he attempts to include the Irish and Christian gods and angels, a complicated system of linking colours, planets, the tonal scale, numbers, and metals. Also in this diary is Yeats's first written definition of Solar vision (objectivity) versus Lunar vision (subjectivity), a concept which was to become a basic part of a *A Vision* twenty-five years later.

The manuscript of rituals and the diary may strike us as overelaborate, but they offer conclusive evidence that in 1889 Yeats was fascinated by the concept of quaternity. He seems to be practicing and learning unfamiliar material, material he did not take from Blake but found Blake using too. What Yeats was working out for a Cabbalistic order, what had been introduced to him by Theosophy and magical study, was also the base of a great poet's symbolic structure – at least as Yeats perceived it. He never gave up the concept of quaternity once he had accepted it; it was to affect not only his philosophy, but also his poetic theory and practice.

Though Yeats was accurate in his ideas about the base of Blake's system, he made a revealing error in his summation of Blake in the 1893 edition. He recognizes Blake's belief that everything once united by the 'Universal Mind' was divided after the Fall and is now at war. But so strongly had he begun to believe in himself that he stresses that the Universal Mind was once 'clairvoyant'.[25] Yeats sees that to Blake, the imagination is a symbol for Christ and vice versa, but then goes on to say: 'In Imagination only we find a human faculty that touches nature on one side, and spirit on the other'.[26] This represents a definite misunderstanding of

Blake, for whom nature was evil; it is a solidly Yeatsian concept. The definition of the imagination he gives here follows not Blake but Coleridge and concisely pressages Yeats's own beliefs and those of Wallace Stevens, who would write: 'Reality is life and life is society and the imagination and reality; that is to say, the imagination and society are inseparable'.[27]

Stevens's 'society' and 'life' are Blake's 'Nature' and for Stevens as for Yeats, the imagination encompasses all. Yeats may share Blake's hatred of reason and abstraction but even in 1893, he does not divide gnostically. In fact, Blake's ability to divide good from evil confuses the young Yeats:

> Blake's peculiar use of the word 'evil' often causes obscurity, for he does not always take the trouble to say when he restricts his meaning to what 'the religious' so call. . . . Blake wrote on the fly leaf of 'Divine Love and Wisdom', 'There is not good will. Will is always evil'.[28]

Blake is far from obscure in his use of the word 'evil'; all will is evil for Blake. Yeats cannot believe this and so dismisses it as 'obscure'.

Besides recognizing the concept of quaternity and being confused on the matter of good and evil in Blake, Yeats sought supportive evidence for his own ideas on quaternity, good, and evil. In 'The Necessity of Symbolism', he refers to 'this poetic genius or central mood in all things. . . .'[29] and goes on to define it thus:

> As mood differs from mood, and emotion from emotion . . . it will be seen that there is something common to them all – a mood that goes through all the moods. This is what Blake means when he speaks of 'the poetic genius', as he sometimes does, as if there were but one genius for all men. . . . When . . . we allow our imagination to expand . . . we become vehicles for the universal thought and merge in the universal mood.[30]

Bloom is correct in pointing out that Yeats misinterpreted Blake's intention and that 'moods' belongs to Yeats (and Pater) and not to Blake.[31] What is most important, however, is not the misunderstanding itself but how Yeats goes on to use it. Yeats is twisting Blake's concept of 'poetic genius' to make it equal with what he earlier called 'the Universal Mind'. He refuses to admit that for Blake the Universal Mind is now divided and at war. In forging his own base, he observes that:

No man can see or think of anything that has not affinity with his mood or 'state', as Blake preferred to call it. The materialist sees only what belongs to his contracted consciousness. The creative visionary or man of genius has all the thoughts, symbols, and experiences that enter within his larger circle. If he has developed his perception of mental sound it will give him music; if his perception of thought, philosophic generalizations; and if his sense of mental sight, visions, strong or faint, according to his power of concentration upon them. The mood of the seer, no longer bound in by the particular experiences of his body, spreads out and enters into the particular experiences of an ever-widening circle of other lives and beings, for it will more and more grow one with that portion of the mood essence which is common to all that lives. The circle of individuality will widen out until other individualities are contained within it, and their thoughts, and the persistent thought-symbols which are their spiritual or mental bodies, will grow visible to it. He who has thus passed into the impersonal portion of his own mind perceives that it is not a mind but all minds.[32]

Here Yeats moves away from Blake to a short step from his later concept of *Anima Mundi*. He does not yet see the universal mind encompassing not only all that lives but also all that has lived; for the present he merely states, in contradiction of Blake, that the universal mind is alive and undivided. When we remember that it was at exactly this time that Yeats was first recognizing his own 'sense of mental sight' – experiencing his first visions, some strong, some faint – we recognize Yeats as 'the man of genius'. Describing this period in his own life he tells us of experiments with the symbols taught him by the Cabbalists:

When two people, between whose minds there was even a casual sympathy, worked together under the same symbolic influence, the dream or reverie would divide itself between them, each half being the complement of the other; and now and again these complementary dreams, or reveries, would arise spontaneously.[33]

There is no way we will ever know whether Yeats deliberately swerved from Blake's beliefs. Neither of the two major concepts he saw in Blake, quaternity and the universal mind, were new to him and this indicates that his reading was strongly influenced by ideas of his own which were in embryo state rather than by a conscious *clinamen*. Years later, he still held to the idea that:

The four quarters of London represented Blake's four great mythological personages, the Zoas, and also the four elements.

These few sentences were the foundation of all study of the philosophy of William Blake that requires an exact knowledge for its pursuit and that traces the connection between his system and that of Swedenborg and of Boehme.[34]

Yeats did not continue to hold that Blake believed in the universal mind as a living thing. In the end, he found verification of quaternity the idea most useful to him in the making of great poetry.

So much has been written about what Yeats took from Blake, about their similarities and differences, that it has been overlooked that there was a point, even when he was writing his commentary, at which Yeats began to consciously mark Blake as, if not wrong, at least limited. In what Bloom sees as Yeats collapsed into ridiculous Cabbalism, we can see the beginning of his negative reactions to Blake: Yeats writes:

> In *Br* the *br* is made evident. They belong to dark anger.... But in this latter name [Ololon] the *l* is not a letter of darkness, and it alternates with the *o* as Ololon (who contained multitudes of both sexes) [who] alternates her moods till she manifests as a virgin at last, just as her name closes with the letter of night.[35]

Yeats was trying rather desperately to explain what bothered him most about Blake – his covering of his system by a 'peculiar use of synonyms'.[36] His attempt to explain Blake's terminology caused him to reach, and in his reaching he tells us much about his growing concern for language itself. As much as he respects Blake's achievement, Yeats is uncomfortable with the verbal 'covering' of the poems.[37]

In 1897, four years after the Ellis-Yeats edition was published, Yeats wrote 'William Blake and the Imagination', and 'William Blake and His Illustrations to *The Divine Comedy*'. By that time he had sifted most of his opinions about Blake and they changed little afterwards. Reinforcing what he hinted in the edition, Yeats begins the first essay by saying:

> There have been men who loved the future like a mistress, and the future mixed her breath into their breath and shook her hair about them, and hid them from the understanding of their times. William Blake was one of these men, and *if he spoke confusedly and obscurely* it was because he spoke of things for whose speaking he could find no models in the world he knew.[38]

In the well-wrought metaphor of the future, Yeats offers perhaps the most respectful apologia possible for a critic who finds Blake's speech sometimes obscure and confused. It is his remaining central objection after his four years of work on the edition. He remains encouraged that Blake 'learned from Jacob Boehme and from old alchemist writers that imagination was the first emanation of divinity . . . and . . . that the imaginative arts were therefore the greatest of Divine revelations'.[39] Foreshadowing his own later belief, he asserts that for Blake, at least intellectually, 'Passions, because most living, are most holy'.[40] It is in this statement and in his fondness for Blake's engraving, 'Francesca and Paolo',[41] that we can see Yeats's developing attitude toward sexuality. As before with the poetry, he interprets the engraving to indicate Blake's complete empathy with and understanding of the plight of the two lovers. He wished to believe he had Blake's agreement that sex was a microcosmic representation of a divine, creative act.[42] As he moved away from Blake, he attempted to find a congenial idea of love not in the poetry but in the engravings.

What stands out in Yeats's experience with Blake is that though the period when he was most involved in finding his own subject matter coincides with the period of work on the edition, the important concepts he takes from Blake concern pattern and systemic structure – form rather than content. When he heralds Blake as 'the first writer of modern times to preach the indissoluble marriage of all great art with symbol',[43] he is close to the definition he was to state in 1898 in 'Symbolism in Painting'. There he says that a symbol is 'The sign or representation of any moral thing by the images or properties of natural things', and goes on to trace this idea not only to Blake but to ' "the things below are as the things above" of the Emerald Tablet of Hermes!'[44] He further links his definition to magic saying:

> All art that is not mere story-telling, or mere portraiture is symbolic, and has the purpose of these symbolic talismans which mediaeval magicians made with complex colours and forms, and bade their patients ponder over daily, and guard with holy secrecy; for it entangles, in complex colours and forms, a part of the Divine Essence.[45]

When Yeats slides away from Blake it is always in the direction of his experience with the learning from Theosophy and Cabbalism. Here he is, in fact, far from Blake who had no intention to use the 'things below' to represent the 'things above' in accord with the Smaragdine Tablet; similarly, Blake's invention of a verbal system of reference had little connection with conventional English. In these essays, what is significant to our understanding of Yeats's work is his definition of symbols and art, and their connection with magic. His 1897-98 definition is the thread from which he will weave the fabric of his later theories.

Once we see the pattern of Yeats's misunderstanding and shifts from Blake during the period when he was most involved with Blake's work, we again confront a problem that has vexed critics from Frye to Adams. As Adams states it, Ellis and Yeats 'ran afoul of the word "mysticism" '[46] in their commentary. He elaborates by pointing out that Yeats's assertion that 'the chief difference between the metaphors of poetry and the symbols of mysticism is that the latter are woven together into a complete system', simply won't 'survive scrutiny'.[47] Yeats's assertion not only will survive but deserves scrutiny if we are to understand his final judgment of Blake. The solidity and coherence of the myth which initially amazed Yeats, as well as the obscure language in which it was couched, led him finally to say of Blake that:

> The limitation of his view was from the very intensity of his vision; he was a too literal realist of imagination, as others are of nature; and because he believed that the figures seen by the mind's eye, when exalted by inspiration, were 'eternal existences', symbols of divine essences, *he hated every grace of style that might obscure their lineaments.*[48]

This judgment, though he makes it here of Blake's illustrations, is the same one he applies to Blake's poetry. It is strikingly similar to the judgment he made of George Russell, whom he thought had surrendered himself to his visions and thus diminished his art. Though Yeats always regarded Blake as a great poet and a positive influence on him, it was partially because he never gave up some important misunderstandings of his precursor. But, he always called Blake a mystic, long after he had firmly made the distinction between the mystic (one who submits his will to a system or vision) and the magician (one who controls and uses his will to create new possibilities for apprehension and understanding). Like Stevens after him, Yeats perceived, as early as 1898, that to be 'too literal a realist of imagination' was as dangerous as to be too literal a realist of nature. Both literalisms, when used exclusively, diminish the possibilities for communication because the symbols (in poetry it will be the words themselves) will be obscure. Style – form – will be intricately and importantly bound up with Yeats's subject matter; he will strive always for language that will not cloud the lineaments of his vision. The problem is that language that is tied to a system will be insufficiently *resonant* – too tight, *literal*. He will attempt the role of magician, rejecting firmly that of mystic.

Yeats called Blake his teacher and perhaps the most important lesson he learned from him was how not to write. Above all, he sought an audience – he sought to communicate. For Yeats, and for us, this is the crucial difference between the two poets. He learned first from Blake that if he was to write from a mythology he must not write obscurely. He learned that to submit totally to one's vision could limit not only a Russell but also a great poet like Blake. What he saw as Blake's three commands for engraving, he was to apply to his own poetry: '. . . seek a determinate outline . . . avoid a generalised treatment, and . . . desire always abundance and exuberance. . . .'[49]

If we compare the poetry from the 1889 *Crossways* with that of the 1893 *The Rose*, we see Yeats beginning to use his new knowledge. He starts the effort which will preoccupy him throughout the 'nineties (and, indeed, for the rest of his career), moving away from the soft heaviness of lines like

> 'Your eyes that once were never weary of mine
> Lie now half hidden under pendulous lids,
> Because our love is waning.'[50]

By 1893, not only has his diction begun to be more determinate, but he is also consciously addressing his audience, Ireland in the coming times, to which he says:

> While still I may, I write for you . . .
> That you, in the dim coming times,
> May know how my heart went with them
> After the red-rose-bordered hem.[51]

Though he had not found a style he could regard as truly his own, he was gaining confidence and clarifying the basic ideas about poetic form and about his subject matter that were to carry him from the 'nineties into the twentieth century.

NOTES

[1] Hazard Adams, *Blake and Yeats: The Contrary Vision* (New York: Russell and Russell, 1955), p. xiii.

[2] Harold Bloom, *Yeats* (New York: Oxford University Press, 1970).

[3] Bloom's implication here is that *A Vision* and its allied poems and plays are also nonsense. He is stating an opinion which becomes starkly clear later in *Yeats*—that only Yeats's early poetry is valuable and that the late poetry, judged by most as Yeats's greatest, is hardly worth discussion except to point out the nonsense of most of it.

[4] *Yeats*, p. 77.

[4a] *Ibid*.

[5] W. B. Yeats, *Autobiographies* (London: Macmillan, 1966), p. 114.

[6] Allan Wade, ed., *The Letters of W. B. Yeats* (London: Hart-Davis, 1955), p. 112. Hereafter referred to as *Letters*.

[7] The rest of the volume seems to be mainly the work of Ellis, who Yeats later characterized as a man whose 'conversation would often pass out of my comprehension, or indeed, I think, of any man's, into a labyrinth of abstraction and subtlety and then suddenly return with some verbal conceit or turn of wit'. *Autobiographies*, p. 163. The work of Ellis when writing on Blake seldom returns to comprehensible areas and shows few conceits or turns of wit.

[8] Edwin Ellis and W. B. Yeats, eds., *The Works of William Blake* (London: Bernard Quaritch, 1893), I, ix. Hereafter referred to as the Ellis-Yeats edition.

[9] *Ibid*.

[10] *Autobiographies*, p. 270.

[11] Ellis-Yeats, I, ix.

[12] *Ibid*., I, 235.

[13] W. B. Yeats, *Essays and Introductions* (London: Macmillan, 1961), p. 330.

[14] Recounted in the introduction to *The Poems of William Blake*, ed. W. B. Yeats (London: Routledge and Kegan Paul, Ltd., 1905).

[15] *Letters*, p. 872.

[16] *Poems of Blake*, p. xvi.

[17] *Ibid*., pp. xx-xxi.

[18] Ellis-Yeats, I, p. xiii.

[19] *Ibid*.

[20] Ellis-Yeats, I, p. viii.

[21] Ellis-Yeats, II, introduction.

[22] *Letters*, pp. 823-824.

[23] National Library of Ireland MS. 13, 568.

[24] National Library of Ireland MSS. 13, 569; 13, 570; and 13, 574.

[25] Ellis-Yeats, I, xii.

[26] *Ibid*.

[27] Wallace Stevens, *The Necessary Angel* (New York: Vintage, 1951), p. 28.

[28] Ellis-Yeats, I, 241.

[29] *Ibid.*
[30] Ellis-Yeats, I, 241-242.
[31] *Yeats*, pp. 71-72.
[32] Ellis-Yeats, p. 244.
[33] *Autobiographies*, p. 259.
[34] *Ibid.*
[35] Ellis-Yeats, I, 331. Also quoted in *Yeats*, p. 79.
[36] Ellis-Yeats, I, viii.
[37] I must add parenthetically that the dissection of Ololon into syllables does not seem to be totally unperceptive. The source of Blake's terminology is utterly obscure and by suggesting a kind of onomatopeia Yeats may be guessing in a way most of us would not have dared. Again, he is at least telling us how much the weight of an individual letter, or syllable, or word will mean to him.
[38] *Essays and Introductions*, p. 111. Emphasis mine.
[39] *Essays and Introductions*, p. 112.
[40] *Ibid.*, p. 113.
[41] Yeats mentions this plate as the best of Blake's illustrations to Dante in 1887. In 1902, he asked A. H. Bullen to make a print of the 'Francesca and Paolo' for a frontispiece to *Ideas of Good and Evil*. See *Letters*, p. 377.
[42] For another very different analysis of Yeats's interpretation of Blake's attitude toward sex and love, see Bloom's *Yeats*, pp. 75-77. I cannot agree with Bloom that Yeats thought of love and sex as demonic. Bloom's argument in this case is again based on his belief that Yeats was a Gnostic. *As* Bloom defines that term, Yeats simply was not a Gnostic.
[43] *Essays and Introductions*, p. 116.
[44] *Ibid.*, p. 146.
[45] *Ibid.*, p. 148.
[46] *Blake and Yeats*, p. 48.
[47] *Ibid.*, p. 49.
[48] *Essays and Introductions*, pp. 119-120. Emphasis mine.
[49] *Ibid.*, p. 123.
[50] First printed in *Wanderings* (1889); revised for *Works* (1906); from which the text for the definitive edition (1956) was taken; appears in definitive edition, pp. 15-18.
[51] First printed in *The Countess Cathleen* (1892); reprinted in *Poems* (1895); appears in definitive edition (1956), pp. 49-50.

Chapter III

Yeats and Ireland:
The Search for an Identity through Politics, Magic and Mythology

It has been necessary to turn from Yeats's *Autobiographies* to examine the place of Theosophy, Indian thought, and Blake in his development. These topics are treated only briefly in his official remembrances of the 'nineties, the formative period in his life. A more important place in his *Autobiographies* is taken by his account of his attempts to define the place of Ireland, its folklore, mythologies, and politics, in his poetry and in his life. As early as 1887, he had begun work on an edition of Irish *Fairy and Folk Tales* (1888). As he saw it later, he did the work for his 'own purposes',[1] an assertion made credible by his introduction to the two-volume work, for in it he notes that 'Poetry in Ireland has always been mysteriously connected with magic',[2] Yeats's main source for subject matter, for synthesizing his theories about magic and poetry, and for his personal identification was to be Ireland, and from the beginning he was trying to assert the unique connection in Ireland between magic and poetry.

During the 'nineties, he firmly established his identity as an Irish poet and attempted to influence his country toward the unity of culture he saw as so important. Politics and Ireland became the arena in which Yeats was to exercise the magical effects of poetry. And it was during these years that he began to refine his ideas about magic and its power. Magic began to mean not the manipulation of physical reality, but rather a kind of control over self which makes possible a control over events. Pursuing this notion, he established a personal Irish political mythology in which the central figures were John O'Leary and, more importantly, Charles Stewart Parnell. What Yeats admired most in these men, as we will see in the *Autobiographies*, was their individual senses of dignity and self-control, a dignity and control which he saw as a source of power which he wished to emulate. In the 'nineties, he sought to connect politics, magic, poetry and Ireland and to establish himself as the kind of powerful figure who could revitalize the culture through the unifying intensity of his poetry which would draw upon the forces of magic.

But Yeats's path toward definition and assertion was not straight. By 1889, he had identified his subject matter with Ireland; by 1893, he addressed Ireland as his audience, and throughout the 'nineties he was to work and hope for an order of Celtic mysticism. However, his definition of Ireland as a place, his relationship to it as a poet and political figure, and his use of its folklore and mythology is complex. The only times Yeats speaks directly to us in his *Autobiographies,* the statements concern his attitudes toward poetry, or more often, poetry and magic. Throughout *The Trembling of the Veil* we see Yeats obliquely, as he defines himself against the personalities and concerns of others in his life. This was perhaps the way he saw himself – as a man who did not quite belong to Ireland, to any one literary or political movement, or to any specific class.

Yeats was Anglo-Irish. Celtic mythology and magic affected him unconsciously from his youth, and during his adult life it was a conscious and vital element in his poetics, but he was not a Celt. His ancestors were all from England – part of the conquering nation which politically, economically and socially exploited the nation into which he was born and which he was to see as the repository of much that was valuable in the twentieth century. England, the home of his forebears, nearly destroyed the Celts who held the mythology, the legends, and the vision which Yeats celebrated. As an Anglo-Irishman, he never hated England; nor could he think of himself as English. But as much as he identified himself as Irish, he could never accept the real Ireland. In his introduction to *Irish Fairy and Folk Tales,* Yeats criticizes those in Ireland who are too effete to recognize the seriousness and power of folk and fairy beliefs,[3] and later, in a letter to Robert Bridges, he speaks of his book, *The Secret Rose* (1887), saying:

> The book (*The Secret Rose*) has on the whole been very well reviewed and there is talk of its being translated into French. It is at any rate an honest attempt towards that aristocratic esoteric Irish Literature which has been my chief ambition. We have a literature for the people but nothing yet for the few. . . .[4]

For all his concern for a common and simple language, a concern which will shape and mark his later work, Yeats sought his audience, wisely perhaps, among the few, the protestant, Anglo-Irish gentry. From the beginning, though his family was impecunious at best, he sought to identify himself with the Big-House families of Ireland. But Yeats belonged to that tradition no more than he belonged to the old Irish, Catholic class which dominated (and dominates) the country.

But it was the Anglo-Irish of the South, including Yeats himself, who culturally and politically supported the Irish and, as Yeats so often pointed out, led Ireland, from the eighteenth century on, in the struggle for freedom from England. More importantly, for Yeats, the Anglo-Irish led Ireland from the eighteenth century in philosophy and literature. Not until James Joyce, did Ireland produce from its native Celtic stock a giant in literature to rival Swift, Burke, Berkeley and Yeats himself.

Concerned primarily with Yeats as a political figure, Conor Cruise O'Brien notes at length the problem of his 'Anglo-Irish Predicament'.[5] O'Brien asserts that:

> The Irish Protestant stock from which Yeats came was no longer a ruling class but still a superior caste, and thought of itself in this way. When he wrote towards the end of his life of 'the caste system that has saved the intellect of India' he was almost certainly thinking not so much of India as of Ireland. His people were in the habit of looking down on their Catholic neighbours – the majority of those among whom they lived – and this habit Yeats never entirely lost. But when he went to school in England Yeats was to find, as Parnell and others had found, that this distinction had lost much of its validity. Unsophisticates – including all the young – made no more distinction between 'Protestant Irish' and 'Catholic Irish' than they did between Brahmin and untouchable.

O'Brien's statement reflects more than a touch of bitterness; he is satisfied that Yeats, Parnell and the others, should have found themselves scorned in England as Irishmen and set apart in Ireland as Anglo-Irish. But his observation is accurate. Yeats and the other Anglo-Irish were neither Irish nor British: being both, they were fully accepted by neither country.

And so, caught in the Anglo-Irish problem, Yeats identified himself with an Ireland created from his own mind and, in a fierce and ultimately unsentimental fashion, loved the Ireland he had created. In remembering the years 1887–1891, he draws a distinction between Ireland and England acutely and unforgettably:

> In London I saw nothing good and constantly remembered that Ruskin had said to some friend of my father's 'As I go to my work at the British Museum I see the faces of the people

become daily more corrupt'. I convinced myself for a time that on the same journey I saw but what he saw. Certain old women's faces filled me with horror, faces that are no longer there, or if they are pass before me unnoticed: the fat, blotched faces, rising above double chins, of women who have drunk too much beer and eaten too much meat. In Dublin I had often seen old women walking with erect heads and gaunt bodies, talking to themselves with loud voices, mad with drink and poverty, but they were different, they belonged to romance. Da Vinci had drawn women who looked so, and so carried their bodies.[6]

Though this borders on romanticism, like much of Yeats's early poetry, he snatches the passage as it veers toward that edge by his awareness that it was his own perception which shaped the images he saw and by his choice of the unconventional images of the women. His objection to England – represented here by the metaphor of the fat, blotched, disembodied faces – is based on its materialism, its lack of a tradition with which he could identify and respect. Ireland – represented not just by faces but also by the gaunt bodies of the women – belongs to the tradition of Da Vinci – beauty, strength, romance, violence, and a kind of courage. Yeats's Ireland was yet to be destroyed by science and materialism.

Having made Ireland *his* place, Yeats hoped for and demanded the best from it. From the beginning, he rejected 'convivial Ireland with the traditional tear and smile'.[7] In 1892 he wrote to Katharine Tynan:

No poetry has a right to live merely because it is good. It must be The Best of Its Kind. The Best Irish poets are this, and every writer of imagination who is true to himself absolutely may be so.[8]

It was a conviction he was to carry with him: all poets, but Irish poets in particular, should be satisfied with nothing but the best they could produce. He would never tolerate the shoddy rhetoric which justified any literary effort as a success merely because it was written by an Irishman. Experience would temper Yeats's dreams but his conviction that Ireland should represent excellence persisted.

When he served as a Senator in the first six years of the Irish Free State, Yeats spoke often and revealingly. Arguing against censorship, for example, or against the bill which refused to grant or to recognize divorce, he identified himself with both Ireland's Celtic traditions and the Anglo-Irish class. He argued in the Senate for an enlightened policy of restoration of the Gaelic language and in connection with this he spoke to the Irish Literary Society on November 30, 1925. Arguing for a bilingual culture which recognized English as the dominant language, he supported the restoration and preservation of the Gaelic tradition in translation (the way he learned it), hoping that Gaelic would not be compulsory and that it would not eliminate the best of the Anglo-Irish and English tradition from the consideration of the free Irish. In his speech, 'The Child and the State', he said:

> In Gaelic literature we have something that the English-speaking countries have never possessed – a great folk literature. We have in Berkeley and in Burke a philosophy on which it is possible to base the whole life of a nation. That, too, is something which England, great as she is in modern scientific thought and every kind of literature, has not, I think. The modern Irish intellect was born more than two hundred years ago when Berkeley defined in three or four sentences the mechanical philosophy of Newton, Locke and Hobbes, the philosophy of England in his day, and I think of England up to our day, and wrote after each 'We Irish do not hold with this', or some like sentence.[9]

Folk literature, Berkeley and Burke would create an Ireland 'reborn, potent, armed and wise'.[10] Yeats did not prevail against the Catholic majority in the first two Irish Senates. But by the time he gave his senate speeches Yeats knew well what he had only begun to suspect in the 'nineties – that he was a representative of a minority which had no intellectual, spiritual or political place in the Ireland of his time.

In the 'nineties his perceptions of Irish mythologies deepened and sharpened partially because of his position as an Anglo-Irishman and partially because of his experience with Theosophy and Cabbalism. He had spent much of his youth in the West of Ireland with evidences of the Celtic tradition a part of daily life; but he did not begin to see how he could use that tradition until his researches in the occult tradition and in Blake had taught him the correspondences between Celtic mythologies and all old mythologies. For the first few years of his career, Yeats was an Irish poet on one hand, and a poet interested in magic and the occult on the other. Beginning in 1889, he began to integrate his interests and goals, attempting to become one man – an Irish poet, using Irish subject matter, welding into his technique and statements the substance of magic and mythology.

As he would have us see it in his *Autobiographies*, Yeats responded even to Madame Blavatsky because she resembled 'a sort of old Irish peasant woman with an air of humour and audacious power'.[11] It is more likely that he saw later that in her beliefs, as much as in her appearance, Blavatsky resembled the Irish peasants he visited with Lady Gregory – the peasants who told him the stories from which he later constructed his own *Mythologies*. In the last paragraphs of 'Four Years: 1887–1891', Yeats sets the theme he will examine and re-examine in the four remaining books of *The Trembling of the Veil* – his attempt to create a literature for Ireland, from Ireland, that would make the Irish '. . . the first in Europe to seek a unity as deliberately as it had been sought by the theologian, poet, sculptor, architect, from the eleventh to the thirteenth century'.[12] He wondered if he might not '. . . create some new *Prometheus Unbound*; Patrick or Columcille, Oisin, or Finn, in Prometheus' stead; and instead of Caucasus, Cro-Patrick or Ben Bulben?'[13] His hope was that he might create a literature associated with 'music, speech, and dance', which might, at last, 'so deepen the political passion of the nation that all, artist and poet, craftsman and day-labourer would accept a common design'.[14] All this might be possible he believed because as he said:

> Nations, races and individual men are unified by an image, or bundle of related images, symbolical or evocative of the state of mind which is, of all states of mind not impossible, the most difficult to that man, race, or nation; because only the greatest obstacle that can be contemplated without despair rouses the will to full intensity.[15]

So, Yeats would have us believe that from the beginning of the 'nineties, however uncertain his own identity as man and poet, he saw the connections between power, political passion and magic – the will roused to full intensity – and that he envisioned the possibility of recreating that 'bundle of related images' which would unify the culture of Ireland. Some glimmer of these coherent intentions was undoubtedly present in the young Yeats but he could never have stated his dreams so clearly until after he had, at least partially, rejected his grand and equally limited design. Finally, he would seek to create in his poetry the bundle of images capable of unifying and rousing the Western world, not merely Ireland.

In his *Autobiographies*, however, the mature Yeats remembers that as a young artist he hoped to put his ideas about Ireland to work at 'the first lull in politics'.[16] That lull came in 1892 after the death of Parnell when he felt 'a sudden certainty that Ireland was to be like soft wax for years to come'.[17] He had nearly finished work on the Ellis-Yeats edition of Blake and began to devote his energies to the founding of an Irish Literary Society in London, and to the founding of the Young Ireland League in Dublin. He had already become part of the Rhymers' Club which included Ernest Rhys, Lionel Johnson, Ernest Dowson, John Todhunter, Edwin Ellis and Arthur Symons.[18] The literary societies were different from the Rhymers' group, but Yeats's interests and purposes were entwined. He hoped for a series of publications of Irish Literature to be read in England and Ireland. In Ireland, he wanted to see a system of libraries and reading rooms across the country to educate the Irish to their own tradition. In an article published three days before Parnell's death, Yeats described the Young Ireland League idea:

> The actual work before the league is definite enough. Classes will be organized to teach the history and language of Ireland, lectures will be given upon Irish subjects, and most important of all, reading rooms will be started in connection with the various branches.[19]

The scheme waited until May, 1892, to be acted upon, at which time it became the National Literary Society in Dublin. Yeats had stated in the Young Ireland article that the libraries system was necessary because: 'Imagination, and not learning, is the centre of life, and from the direction it takes spring thought and conduct....'[20]

Although Ellmann and others have seen in Yeats's efforts here an attempt to impress Maud Gonne, it is apparent that he was also, as he later expressed it so articulately, attempting to create a culture in Ireland which would reflect the unity he desired and thought necessary to a true political revolution. His motives were seldom single; he probably did wish to impress Maud Gonne, but even more, to create an audience for his own work. He intended to produce the works of the imagination which he believed were 'the centre of life'.

Had his single motive been Maud's favour, he failed rather miserably. Almost from the beginning of his efforts with the literary societies, Yeats was outmanoeuvred by Catholic Irishmen. Though he attempted to arrange publication of shilling copies of Irish books with his publisher, Fisher Unwin, he was replaced in the project by Sir Charles Gavan Duffy. The best he could do, as his letters from the period indicate, was to withdraw with evident grace, having seen his friends, Douglas Hyde and T. W. Rolleston (who was part of the Rhymers' group and head of the London Irish Literary Society), appointed as editors under Duffy.[21] Yeats minimizes the struggle with the literary groups in his *Autobiographies*, but his comments on Duffy evince the anger he felt.

Having demolished Duffy's prose as worse than meaningless, Yeats goes on to say that:

> One imagined his youth in some little gaunt Irish town, where no building or custom is revered for its antiquity; and there speaking a language where no word, even in solitude, is ever spoken slowly and carefully because of emotional implication; and of his manhood of practical politics, of the dirty piece of orange peel in the corner stairs as one climbs up to some newspaper office; of public meetings where it would be treacherous amid so much geniality to speak or even to think of anything that might cause a moment's misunderstanding in one's own party.[22]

Yeats's arrogance serves him here as his irony works to save him from romanticism elsewhere. He hated Duffy and all that Duffy represented – hypocrisy, absence of respect for or understanding of the Irish past full of magic and mythology, ignorance of the power of language, pettiness, dirtiness and parochialism.

In the battle over the books, John O'Leary ranged himself on Yeats's side in the argument, but his support was 'capricious'.[23] John F. Taylor, the famous orator, supported Duffy. Yeats 'was not Taylor's match with the spoken word', being in his own memory 'immature and clumsy'[24] at twenty-seven or twenty-eight. It was not merely Yeats's lack of rhetorical skill or his clumsiness that gave the victory to Duffy and Taylor. They were Catholic, anti-Parnellite, supported by unionists in England and the narrow, provincial group in Dublin; Yeats was Anglo-Irish and Parnellite. It was through the battle of the books that he began to understand his position in Ireland, and out of his realization of himself as outsider grew his vision of Parnell as the first of his solitary, powerful heroes.

O'Leary and Yeats shared a deep respect for Parnell: Yeats tells us,

> Whenever we did not speak of art and letters, we spoke of Parnell. We told each other that he had admitted no man to his counsel; . . . and, above all, we spoke of his pride, that made him hide all emotion while before his enemy. Once he had seemed callous and indifferent to the House of Commons – Forster had accused him of abetting assassination – but when he came among his followers his hands were full of blood, because he had torn them with his nails.[25]

Parnell had, according to Yeats, such 'power over self' that it implied an equal 'expression of the self'. He had, not merely courage and dignity, but also a power over others like that of the magician – as when he held Katharine O'Shea over the sea and she knew that had she moved he would have 'drowned himself and her'. Yeats marvels at Parnell's power, saying that if the country had but understood it, 'What excitement there would have been, what sense of mystery would have stirred in all our hearts, and stirred hearts all through the country. . . .'[26] What he loved in Parnell was the politician's power of self over events and everything he says about Duffy rings with the deepest scorn. And Yeats's hatreds and loves were not to soften with time. Having lost in London and Dublin, he retreated and remembered:

> I was at Sligo when I received a letter from John O'Leary, saying I could do no more in Dublin, for even the younger men had turned against me, were 'jealous', his letter said, though what they had to be jealous of God knows. . . . *I did not yet know that intellectual freedom and social equality are incompatible;* and yet, if I had, could hardly have lived otherwise, being too young for silence. . . . *One must be English or Irish, they would have said.*[27]

Being too young for silence, Yeats plunged again and again into the politics of the 'nineties, though what he hoped for in London and in Dublin was far from merely political.

In October, 1892, he wrote 'Hopes and Fears for Irish Literature'; in it he spoke of the differences between England and Ireland, as he then perceived them:

> In England amongst the best minds, art and poetry are becoming every day more entirely ends in themselves, and all life is made more and more but so much fuel to feed their fire. . . . Poetry is an end in itself; it has nothing to do with thought, nothing to do with philosophy, nothing to do with life, nothing to do with anything but the music of cadence, and beauty of phrase.[28]

Even the young Yeats did not thoroughly accept the 'Art for Art's sake' of Pater or of his English contemporaries, arguing with the Rhymers in London that 'all great art and literature' depend 'upon conviction and upon heroic life'.[29]

In Ireland his problems were reversed: the Irish were 'most interested in the literary forms that gave most opportunity for the display of great characters and great passions'.[30] He found such literature 'often crude and interesting', lamenting that 'side by side with this robustness and rough energy of ours there goes a most utter dreadful intermixture of the commonplace'.³¹ Most of all, he hoped that Irish writers could

> ... learn a little of their [the English] skill, and a little of their devotion to form, a little of their hatred of the commonplace and the banal [in order to] ... make all these restless energies of ours alike the inspiration and the theme of a new and wonderful literature.³²

At other times, Yeats hoped English poets, especially the Rhymers, could seize some of the vitality from the Irish, as he wished the Irish could learn about form from them.

The problems he records in 'Hopes and Fears for Irish Literature' belonged as much to him as to the 'Irish' or to the 'English'; he, after all, was both, and his own poetry of the 'nineties reflects more of the English problem than the Irish one. In the face of his rejection by Catholic, political Ireland, he sought to affirm in several ways his Irish status. '*We* have behind *us* the most moving legends and a history full of lofty passions', he writes.

> If we can but take that history and those legends and turn them into dramas, poems, and stories full of the living soul of the present, and make them massive with conviction and profound with reverie, we may deliver that new great utterance for which the world is waiting.... 'Know thyself' is a true advice for nations as well as for individuals. We must know and feel our national faults and limitations no less than our national virtues, and care for things Gaelic and Irish, not because we hold them better than things Saxon and English, but *because they belong to us, and because our lives are to be spent among them, whether they be good or evil.*³³

This valuable document reveals that Yeats, in 1892 – not quite twenty-eight years old and some distance from his mature poetry – was sure of what he would draw from the English tradition (form, or the concern for form) and from the Celtic tradition (subject matter, the moving legends, the mythology). He tells us not so much what we will find in the Irish Renaissance as a whole but what we will find in his work. He will attempt in the next few years to begin to know himself and his Ireland, with its profound legends, poetic traditions, and history of the Celtic past. Through self-knowledge, understanding Celtic mythology and several other mythologies, by continuing to study personalities, magic, and the forms of language, Yeats will build his own confidence and try for the 'new great utterance' for which he was sure the world waited.

In the years between 1892 and 1897, as he struggled to make Ireland belong to him, Yeats came to know and learn much from John O'Leary, the Fenian leader, who not only supported him in the battle with Duffy but shared his home with him and regularly lent him money. A typical letter fromYeats to O'Leary in these years reads:

> Dear Mr O'Leary, will you be so good as to help me out of a difficulty? There is still £2-3-10 owing to Kegan Paul on *Oisin* and they threaten me with lawyers. . . . I want you to lend me £2-10-0 so that I can make the transfer at once.[34]

As typical were the letters explaining repayment problems:
On May 26, 1896, Yeats wrote:

> Dear Mr O'Leary: Please send me your address as I am anxious to send you the money I have owed you for so long. £6 is if I remember rightly the amount.[35]

In June or July the same year, he wrote:

> My Dear Mr O'Leary: I did not send you the money before because Smithers, the publisher of the *Savoy*, was short of funds and asked me to wait: and I send only £3.5.0 now because I am short in my turn. I could have sent you the whole sum when I wrote first but now I must wait a little before sending the remainder.[36]

Letters like these are embarrassingly common up to 1897, when Yeats met Lady Gregory, who supplanted O'Leary as his main source of loans. Yeats does not, for understandable reasons, mention O'Leary's function as financier in the *Autobiographies*, but what he does tell us is perhaps more important. O'Leary told him accurately that 'In this country, . . . a man must have upon his side the Church or the Fenians, and you will never have the Church'.[37] It prepared Yeats for some of the opposition he would face because of his Anglo-Irish background and shored up his emerging nationalism. Generally, the Fenian leader served as a father not only to the movement but also to Yeats himself. O'Leary was stable, Nationalist, and Conservative at the same time. It was from this source, more than any other, that Yeats took his political opinions.

O'Leary abhorred assassination and bombing as tactics, advocating dignity above all else. As Yeats's feelings about Duffy emerge in his description of his enemy's past, so do his feelings about O'Leary become clear in his description of his surrogate father:

> His ancestors had probably kept little shops, or managed little farms in County Tipperary, yet he hated democracy, though he never used the word either for praise or blame, with more than feudal hatred. . . . He had no philosophy, but things distressed his palate, and two of those things were international propaganda and the Organized state, . . . nor could he speak such words as 'philanthropy', 'humanitarianism', without showing by his tone of voice that they offended him. The Church pleased him little better, . . . he would say, 'My religion is the Old Persian, to pull the bow and tell the truth'.[38]

Yeats loved O'Leary for his opinions, for his help, and most of all, for his courage. He remembered O'Leary's saying, 'There are things a man must not do to save a nation': and when he asked what things, O'Leary said, 'To cry in public'. Yeats added: 'and I think it probable that he would have added, if pressed, "To write oratorical or insincere verse" '.[39] Yeats built O'Leary into his living mythology as he did Parnell, Lady Gregory and Synge. He assumes himself in total sympathy with O'Leary in his confident assertion that insincere or rhetorical verse would equal crying in public. We will never know if O'Leary believed that; but we know Yeats did.

Yeats came to share O'Leary's hatred of formless democracy, humanitarianism – or any 'ism' – and the organized Church. He wanted his work to reflect the courage he saw in the friends he immortalised. O'Leary provided the living link with Nationalist Ireland that Yeats so needed in the 'nineties. It is possible that the amount of time he spent in London and Paris, the involvement with Cabbalism which continued through these years might have made him an exile such as Wilde and Joyce became. In 1895, he wrote to Katharine Tynan,

> . . . when I am tired, this endless war with Irish stupidity gets on my nerves. Either you or I could have had more prosperous lives probably, if we left Ireland alone and went our way on the high seas. . . .[40]

But the support of O'Leary, combined with Yeats's growing interest in the folklore of Ireland as a source for his own mythology, served to maintain his link to Ireland.

In 'Ireland after Parnell', one other man besides O'Leary

emerges as a positive force in Yeats's life and work: Douglas Hyde. Hyde had helped Yeats by providing him tales for his *Irish Fairy and Folk Tales* and continued to be his main source of information on Ireland's folklore until 1897 when he met Lady Gregory and began visiting the people of Western Ireland for himself. Hyde had learned Gaelic, unlike Yeats, and had written poetry in Gaelic which was popular with the people before Yeats met him.[41] For many years, Hyde was to be a more popular figure than Yeats – his Gaelic pen-name, Craoibhin Aoibhin,[42] was worn as a nationalist sign embroidered on hatbands.

Yeats much respected Hyde during the early years of the 'nineties. He reviewed Hyde's *Beside the Fire: A Collection of Irish Gaelic Folk Stories* for the *National Observer* in 1891, praising it for its method (Hyde printed the Gaelic on one side with the English translation facing) and its beauty. He compares the beliefs Hyde had found to those of Swedenborg and Coleridge – the language to 'the simple fancifulness of childhood'.[43] Above all, Yeats was impressed with and no doubt learned from Hyde's use of his own imagination in the retelling of the folk tales. Yeats railed against 'scientific' folk-lore which treated what he considered living things as specimens not to be felt or allowed to penetrate the present. Hyde was, at least until 1893, Yeats's 'Ideal Folklorist'. 'A tale told by him is quite as accurate as any "scientific" person's rendering', Yeats asserts, noting his 'sacred rage' when he comes upon 'some exquisite story, dear . . . from childhood, written out in newspaper English and called science'.[44] Yeats's review of Hyde's *Love Songs of Connacht* (1893) marked the high point in his respect for Hyde's work. 'Dr Hyde's volume of translations, . . .' he tells us, 'is one of those rare books in which art and life are so completely blended that praise or blame become well nigh impossible'.[45]

Though they remained friends, Hyde turned away from his folk-lore, to found first the Gaelic League and then to abandon both scholarship and art to politics, becoming the first president of Ireland from 1938 to 1945. Yeats regretted and disapproved of Hyde's defection from the world of poetry and folklore but never rejected what he learned from him – the possibility of bringing the mythology of Ireland to life in his own language, English. What Hyde did in the early 'nineties, Yeats compared to the preservation of Eastern mythologies:

> . . . I was to stand at his side and listen to Galway mowers singing his Gaelic words without their knowing whose words they sang. It is so in India, where peasants sing the words of the great poet of Bengal without knowing whose words they sing, and it must

often be so where the old imaginative folk-life is undisturbed. . . .⁴⁶

Yeats listened to the songs, read them, and saw again the correspondences between all old mythologies; he also verified for himself what Eliot would later call the social function of poetry. The place where the Folk-life was most undisturbed in all of Europe was Ireland, and that was where Yeats would look for his own key to the past, the key that would make the past present, and perhaps shape the future – in any case, his future. As a poet with ambitions to make a 'new great utterance', Yeats depended on what he could make of the Celtic past for two main reasons: first, his interests and beliefs had directed him toward finding a kind of Ur-mythology from the time when he first discovered the correspondences between Indian, Hermetic, Theosophic, and Blakean thought; second, and of equal importance, was his position as an outsider in contemporary Ireland, his position as an Anglo-Irishman. Yeats turned to pre-Christian Celtic mythology for the basis of his subject matter both to root his poetry and his own sense of being an Irish poet; he sought a mythology for his poetry and for himself.

Yeats's earliest attitudes toward 'Irish Fairies' are represented in an article from the *Leisure Hour* (London) of October 1890,⁴⁷ in which he says:

> When I tell people that the Irish peasantry still believe in Fairies, I am often doubted. . . . They do not imagine it possible that . . . any kind of ghost or goblin can live within range of our daily papers. . . . They are quite wrong. The ghosts and goblins so still live and rule in the imaginations of innumerable Irish men and women, and not merely in remote places, but close even to big cities.⁴⁸

An attitude of naïveté, of defensiveness and puckish fun, marks Yeats's voice in this article. He would not often again use 'ghosts and goblins' nor even 'Fairies',⁴⁹ preferring instead, 'Sidhe'. And by 1893, when *The Celtic Twilight* was first published, much of the defensiveness of the stance he takes in 'Irish Fairies' is gone. It was in *The Celtic Twilight* which he continued to revise until 1902, that Yeats began to use Irish mythology as more than a system which 'makes all cats griffens and all human life a sterile pattern'.⁵⁰

The title of *The Celtic Twilight* may be derived from his review of Lady Wilde's *Ancient Curses, Charms and Usages of Ireland* (1890) which Yeats titled 'Tales from the Twilight'.⁵¹ In that review Yeats described the twilight:

The grey of the morning is the Irish Witches' hour, when they gather in the shades of large hares and suck the cattle dry; and the grey morning melancholy runs through the legends of my people. Then it is that this world and the other draw near, and not at midnight upon Brockens amidst the foul revelry of evil souls and in the light of the torches of hell.[52]

The Celtic twilight then represents the hour before dawn, the hour of witches and metamorphosis. But Yeats makes clear the further meaning the twilight time had for him in a poem which grew, as did much of his poetry, out of the prose in his article and in *The Celtic Twilight*. In 'Into the twilight' (1893),[53] he writes:

> Out-worn heart, in a time out-worn,
> Come clear of the nets of wrong and right;
> Laugh, heart, again in the grey twilight,
> Sigh, heart, again in the dew of the morn.
>
> Your mother Eire is always young,
> Dew ever shining and twilight grey;
> Though hope fall from you and love decay,
> Burning in fires of a slanderous tongue.
>
> Come, heart, where hill is heaped upon hill:
> For there the mystical brotherhood
> Of sun and moon and hollow and wood
> And river and stream work out their will;
>
> And God stands winding His lonely horn,
> And time and the world are ever in flight;
> And love is less kind than the grey twilight,
> And hope is less dear than the dew of the morn.

Though this poem was not collected until the 1889 *Wind Among the Reeds*, it was written in the same year *The Celtic Twilight* was published and illuminates not only Yeats's choice of title for the set of tales but also his fascination with the twilight time in the 'nineties. He sought a neutral ground from which to create, and found a metaphor for it in the timeless, magical, grey dawn which was also the time when the Druids practiced their rituals. If he was to escape 'the nets of wrong and right', Yeats saw that he would have to go back to the beginning of Irish culture, the twilight dawn when Ireland was 'Eire'.

But, 'Into the Twilight' is burdened, as is much of Yeats's early poetry, by the melancholy he saw in 'all the legends of my people'. It is in the prose of *The Celtic Twilight* that we see his melancholy begin to lighten. In the stories of that book we see for the first time aspects of his technique, beliefs, and humour that do not appear in the poetry until after the turn of the century.

Though the narrator in the tales of *The Celtic Twilight* seems to be Yeats himself, he states that 'many of the tales in this book were told me by one Paddy Flynn', who possessed the 'visionary melancholy of purely instinctive natures and of all animals'.[54] He carefully defines the melancholy of Paddy Flynn, however: it causes him to ever recommend 'mirth and hopefulness', much like the Irish peasants described in the 'Tales from the Twilight' review who, though they do not lack melancholy, display 'no gloom, no darkness, no love of the ugly, no moping'.[55] Paddy Flynn is fictitious, one of Yeats's own masks; and it is through his voice that we hear what is perhaps the first evidence of the poet's developing sense of irony: Paddy Flynn was fond of telling how Columcille cheered up his mother.[56]

> 'How are you to-day, mother?' said the saint.
> 'Worse', replied the mother. 'May you be worse to-morrow', said the saint. The next day Columcille came again, and exactly the same conversation took place, but the third day the mother said, 'Better, thank God', and the saint replied, 'May you be better to-morrow'.[57]

Yeats suggests for the first time in the repetition of Columcille's[58] treatment of his mother that self-pity and melancholy, perhaps even sickness, are products of the mind and that irony may be the proper cure. (Columcille, at any rate, emerges from the tale as a good psychologist). His growing awareness of the uses of irony is evident in Yeats's recollection of the period during which he wrote the *Celtic Twilight* stories. He tells us:

> I was preparing the way without knowing it for a great satirist and master of irony, for master-works stir vaguely in many before they grow definite in one man's mind, and to help me I had already flitting through my head, jostling other ideas and so not yet established there, a conviction that we should satirize rather than praise, that original virtue arises from the discovery of evil.[59]

The great satirist and master of irony of whom he speaks is John Synge, but Yeats would become as great a satirist and master of irony. He goes on to connect his sense of irony as a major method to his perception that 'original virtue arises from the discovery of evil', saying:

If we [the Irish] were, as I had dreaded, declamatory, loose, and bragging, we were but the better fitted – that declared and measured – to create *unyielding personality, manner at once cold and passionate,* daring long-premeditated act; and if bitter beyond all the people of the world, we might yet lie – that too declared and measured – nearest the honeycomb....[60]

Yeats began to see that irony was more than a simple method for inverting meaning, that through use of ironic vision one could create from one's own personality its opposite consciousness, that, in fact, all extremes created and contained their own opposites. Later he would master for his own poetry the 'at once cold and passionate' manner, but it is in his re-telling of the Irish folk tales that he first employed ironic humour as a tool.

In 'A Remonstrance with Scotsmen for Having Soured the Disposition of their Ghosts and Faeries', Yeats makes clear how much he considers ironic humour a major feature of Irish society. 'In Scotland you are too theological, too gloomy'; he complains, 'You have burnt all the witches. In Ireland we have left them alone'.[61] As an example, he cites the difference in the two cultures' attitudes toward water-goblins and water-monsters. In Scotland the monsters are feared; in Ireland, Yeats tells us, he once caught a large conger eel and told a fisherman that one 'three times larger' had escaped.

'That was him', said the fisherman. 'Did you hear how he made my brother emigrate? My brother was a diver . . . and grubbed stone for the Harbour Board. One day the beast comes up to him, and says, "What are you after?" "Stones, Sur", says he. "Don't you think you had better be going?" "Yes, Sur", says he. And that's why my brother emigrated'.[62]

One of the ways irony functions in this short tale within a tale, is to exploit inversely our lack of belief in the stories of fishermen. We might assume that the brother who emigrated was as frightened of monsters as any Scotsman; but it is respect based upon total acceptance which determines the man's response. For the Irish, Yeats insists, the giant not only exists but commands respect and may be used to explain an actual event, such as the emigration of the fisherman's brother. While the Scots have changed their monster stories to support the terrifying side of Calvinism, the Irish have integrated their monsters into the stream of contemporary life. Through his irony, Yeats suggests that we should not consider all Celtic folk tales in the same way and further, that the tales reflect significant cultural differences.

In *The Celtic Twilight,* Yeats also insists on the benign nature of Irish Faeries. That instance is ironic, for some experiences with them require macabre humour in the retelling. In 'The Kidnappers', he writes:

> There is hardly a valley or mountain-side where they cannot tell you of someone pillaged from amongst them. Two or three miles from the Heart Lake lives an old woman who was stolen away in her youth. After seven years she was brought home again for some reason or other, but she had no toes left. She had danced them off.[63]

The casual 'for some reason or other', combined with the apparent precision of 'two or three miles from the Heart Lake' subtly suggests that the tale is factual but the added information that the woman had danced her toes off indicates that human traffic with the faeries is not always benign in its effects.

Yeats was experimenting in these tales with irony in a way he will not attempt in his poetry until after the turn of the century. Eventually, it will be through the use of irony that he gains complexity and distance on his subject matter. Irony will become a major method of controlling his forms. As Magic came to mean control for Yeats, irony would become more and more important as a formal technique. Here, what we have seen him do follows the same pattern as his encounters with Theosophy and Cabbalism. He uses the Irish folklore as his subject matter and in order to control it, to work it into his system, he does not merely elucidate the tales, but uses them, retelling them his way.

Basically, the effect of the three tales is to establish the cultural importance of the Irish folk beliefs and to illustrate how these beliefs work in concrete situations – sickness, emigration, feet with no toes. In 'Belief and Unbelief', the second tale in *The Celtic Twilight,* a man tells the narrator, and the narrator agrees, that the faeries 'stand to reason'.[64] This idea is reinforced by tales of doubters. In 'The Man and His Boots', a man refuses to believe in ghosts and is literally kicked out of a haunted house by his own boots; in 'Happy and Unhappy Theologians', a Galway man believes the faeries are the children of Satan and sees visions of Hell and Purgatory regularly. He is balanced in the tale by a Mayo woman who believes the faeries are 'people like ourselves, only better looking';[65] she sees nothing but pleasant visions.

'Happy and Unhappy Theologians' goes beyond affirming that it is functional to believe in the Sidhe; it also states a theme Yeats examines throughout the volume – the combination of Catholic and Pagan ideas in the West of Ireland. As he states in 'A Remonstrance with Scotsmen', 'The Catholic religion likes to keep on good terms with its neighbours'.[66] What Yeats saw, before Synge's *Riders to the Sea,* was that the ancient Celtic myths and forms of belief had been basically undisturbed by the introduction of Catholicism to the West of Ireland. The peasants accepted both systems of belief side by side, seeing no contradictions between them, despite the caveats of the official Church.

'Our Lady of the Hills', examines the differences in the attitudes of Catholic and Protestant children toward visions. A Protestant girl dressed in blue and white is seen by a group of Catholic children who take her first to be the Virgin Mary and then a faery. 'Her good protestant heart was greatly troubled',[67] and she tried to explain who she was, talking to them 'a long time about Christ and the apostles'.[68] The children are finally convinced that she is not a vision but respond with an anger she cannot understand. Yeats believed that the element of mysticism in Catholicism encouraged the maintenance of Pagan beliefs; Protestantism, on the other hand, was marked by sterility and narrowness of imagination. What the tale verifies is that Yeats had little love for the Catholic Church, nor for the protestant. What he perceived as important was the difference in the place of imagination under the two systems.

For the nominally Catholic peasants, Heaven, Hell, and Purgatory were very close to their lives, as close as the land of the Sidhe.[69] In April, 1898, Yeats defended his views on this issue in a letter to the editor of the *Outlook*. He had been accused by an anonymous commentator of being 'unable to separate the dreams and poetic fancies from the realities', being trapped in the 'dream of a poetical folk-lorist'. He replied:

> If your paragraphist will consult my article in the January number of the *Nineteenth Century,* . . . he will find that I have been very careful about my facts and have quoted witness after witness. And if your paragraphist, who is, perhaps, a Catholic, will wait until I have completed the series of essays, . . . he will find that the Irish peasant has invented, or that somebody has invented for him, a vague, though not altogether unphilosophical, reconciliation between his Paganism and his Christianity.[70]

Bourgeois Catholics and Protestants earned nothing but Yeats's scorn. The power of imagination he so respected was to be found in the Pagan/Catholic peasants, who were, in his opinion, more connected to ancient Ireland and its beliefs than they were to contemporary Irish Christianity.

In a 1902 addition to *The Celtic Twilight*, he explains why the Western Irish believe as they do:

> ... I am certain that the water, the water of the seas and of lakes and of mist and rain, has all but made the Irish after its image. Images form themselves in our minds perpetually as if they were reflected in some pool. We gave ourselves up in old times to mythology, and saw the gods everywhere. We talked to them face to face, and the stories of that communion are so many that I think they outnumber all the like stories of all the rest of Europe. ... We can make our minds so like still water that beings gather about us that they may see, it may be, their own images, and so live for a moment with a clearer, perhaps even with a fiercer life because of our quiet. Did not the wise Porphyry think that all souls came to be born because of water, and that 'even the generation of images in the mind is from water?'[71]

Though F. A. C. Wilson's argument about Yeats and his conventional sources insists that the poet drew the greater part of his mythologies from Platonism and neo-Platonism, the above passage makes clear that Yeats used orthodox tradition to verify correspondences between mythologies, and not to construct them.[72] Further, Yeats's statement indicates that as he moved back to the 'old times' of mythology he was able to identify himself totally as Irish. His ancestors did not, in fact live in Ireland in the time when the Celts 'saw the gods everywhere', but in his own mythologies, Yeats becomes one with the Celtic people.

Ellmann and Blackmur, among others, have maintained that Yeats did not always believe in the system which he created. But in *The Celtic Twilight* Yeats's stance as narrator makes it possible to trace the nature of his own doubts and reservations about the tales he records and, indeed the system he was building. Among the thirty-nine stories of the book, he intersperses at least nine in which the attitude of the narrator is the focus, and many of the tales reflect his own concerns and experiences. In 'A Visionary', for example, a young man visits the narrator and while there sees a vision of a 'shining winged woman';[73] the narrator questions: 'Is it the influence of some living person who thinks of us, and whose thoughts appear to us in that symbolic form?' The question is Yeats's, and he does not doubt the reality of the vision, but rather its source. In the early 'nineties, Yeats relied on the power of telepathic communication more solidly than he did in visions from beyond the grave – however, this attitude was not static, as his later researches in Spiritualism attest – and the narrator's question is more rhetorical than it is genuinely sceptical. The visionary tells the narrator of a peasant who once burst out with 'God possesses the heavens – God possesses the heavens – but He covets the world'.[75] In the *Autobiographies,* at the end of 'Ireland after Parnell', Yeats attaches four fragments, one of which records that:

> Russell has just come in from a long walk on the Two Rock Mountain, very full of his conversation with an old religious beggar, who kept repeating, 'God possesses the heavens, but He covets the earth – He covets the earth'.[76]

'A Visionary' reflects Yeats's own experience and his own questions but it indicates disbelief less than it does his desire to know the source of visions.

In 'Village Ghosts', the narrator says:

> The Ancient map-makers wrote across unexplored regions, 'Here are lions'. Across the villages of fishermen and turners of the earth, . . . we can write but one line that is certain, 'Here are ghosts'. *My ghosts* inhabit the village of H – – – . . . .[77]

The narrator, despite his seeming certainty which extends to calling the Faeries 'children of Lilith', retreats at the end of the tale to emphasize that he was 'told' the stories. Yeats often adopts the stance of listener/observer in his tales but he does not do so to indicate his own disbelief in what he has heard; it is a technique which subtly reassures a doubtful audience of his 'rationality'.

'The Sorcerers', 'Enchanted Woods', and 'The Old Town', reflect his certainty of the existence of the Sidhe, magic and trances. The narrator is Yeats, as we can see, for instance, in 'The Sorcerers'. The narrator takes part in an experiment in Black Magic which involves cutting the throat of a black cock, burning herbs, and murmuring incantations. The sorcerer falls into a trance state himself, being sure that 'this trance was out of harmony with itself, in other words, evil'.[78] He does not doubt the existence of the trance state, nor the possibility of its being evil. In the second of the four fragments at the end of 'Ireland after Parnell', Yeats recounts the same incident:

> I get in talk with a young man. . . . He is a stranger, but explains that he has inherited magical art from his father, and asks me to his rooms to see it in operation. He and a friend of his kill a black cock, and burn herbs in a big bowl, but nothing happens except that the friend repeats again and again, 'O my God' and

when I ask him why; he has said that he does not know that he has spoken; and I feel that there is something very evil in the room.[79]

Similarly, in 'Enchanted Woods', Yeats says of the Sidhe, 'I say to myself, when I am well out of that thicket of argument, that they are surely there. . . .'[80] He goes on to recount an event from his childhood, also recorded in *Reveries Over Childhood and Youth,* in which he and some companions see lights on a hillside in the darkness. He believes the lights are either 'men and women who lived in earlier times', or 'creatures' who live by the banks of the river.[81]

Believing as he did in the power of visions and of magic, Yeats deliberately wove his own experiences and speculations into the tales of *The Celtic Twilight.* As he had earlier taken from Theosophy and Blake what he could use in his own system, he takes from Irish folk belief what corresponds to his own accumulating set of beliefs, working toward not a set of Irish mythologies, but rather a system of his own mythologies.

How much Yeats was involved in the world of visions and how important they are to him, as early as 1892, is evident in 'The Eaters of Precious Stones'. He tells us of 'waking dreams' he experiences which are 'ever beyond the power of my will to alter in any way'.[82] (Psychology terms these waking dreams 'hypnogogic visions'; they occur immediately preceding or following sleep.) He recounts one of the dream visions important to him:

> One day I saw faintly an immense pit of blackness, round which went a circular parapet, and on this parapet sat innumerable apes eating precious stones out of the palms of their hands. The stones glittered green and crimson, and the apes devoured them with insatiable hunger. I knew that I saw my own Hell there, the Hell of the artist, and that all who sought after beautiful and wonderful things with too avid a thirst, lost peace and form and became shapeless and common.[83]

Placed as it is in *The Celtic Twilight,* 'The Eaters of Precious Stones' testifies to Yeats's deep concern not only to write beautiful poetry but to attain a balance and form which will save him from the shapeless and common hell of the artist. His was not an abstract concern for the proper form for his poetry; it was a deeply embedded determination to seek the experience and the discipline great poetry will require. The final tale in the volume, 'By the Roadside', finds him summing up all he has done, saying,

Folk-Art is, indeed the oldest of the aristocracies of thought, and because it refuses what is passing and trivial, the merely clever and pretty, as certainly as the vulgar and insincere, and because it has gathered into itself the simplest and most unforgettable thoughts of the generations, *it is the soil where all great art is rooted*....[84]

The connections between 'Ireland after Parnell' and the stories of *The Celtic Twilight* indicate that Yeats considered the tales he reworked in 1892 and throughout the 'nineties a most significant task. In recalling the early 'nineties, Yeats undoubtedly consulted these tales to reconstruct his memories. The end of 'Ireland after Parnell' coincides with the time in which he wrote *The Celtic Twilight* and states his understanding of his place in the Irish Renaissance. He will seek a directness of style and employ a sense of irony that his poetry of the 'nineties reflects only in brief flashes. He will continue to study and to use magic, visions, and folklore to make the mythology of Celtic Ireland come alive and reaffirm the power of imagination and hope. Both 'Ireland after Parnell' and *The Celtic Twilight* end with an affirmation of magic and mythology. Magic will be the tool with which to open the Celtic past, make it present, and thus create a great art rooted in the soil of Folk-belief.

NOTES

[1] W. B. Yeats, *Autobiographies* (London: Macmillan, 1966), p. 149.

[2] W. B. Yeats, ed., *Fairy and Folk Tales of the Irish Peasantry* (London: Walter Scott, 1888), p. xii. Published New York 1902 as *Irish Fairy and Folk Tales*.

[3] *Ibid.*, p. xiv.

[4] Allan Wade, ed., *The Letters of W. B. Yeats* (London: Hart-Davis, 1955), p. 286. Hereafter referred to as *Letters*.

[5] Conor Cruise O'Brien, 'Passion and Cunning: An Essay on the Politics of W. B. Yeats,' in *In Excited Reverie*, eds., A. N. Jeffares and K. G. W. Cross (New York: Macmillan, 1965), pp. 207-279.

[6] *Autobiographies*, p. 155.

[7] *Ibid.*, p. 207.

[8] *Letters*, p. 206.

[9] W. B. Yeats, 'The Child and the State', in *The Senate Speeches of W. B. Yeats*, ed., Donald R. Pearce (Bloomington, Indiana: Indiana University Press, 1960), p. 172.

[10] *Ibid.*

[11] *Autobiographies*, p. 173.

12 *Ibid.*, p. 195.
13 *Autobiographies*, p. 194.
14 *Ibid.*
15 *Ibid.*, pp. 194-195.
16 *Ibid.*, p. 199.
17 *Ibid.*
18 *Ibid.*, p. 165.
19 W. B. Yeats, *Uncollected Prose*, ed., John P. Frayne (New York: Columbia University Press, 1970), I, 207.
20 *Ibid.*, I, 208.
21 See Joseph Hone, *W. B. Yeats* (London: Macmillan, 1967), pp. 97ff. for a further discussion of this matter.
22 *Autobiographies*, p. 225.
23 *Ibid.*, p. 227.
24 *Ibid.*
25 *Ibid.*, p. 232.
26 *Ibid.*, p. 233.
27 *Ibid.*, p. 230. Emphasis added.
28 *Uncollected Prose*, I, 248.
29 *Uncollected Prose*, I, 248. Many of Yeats's critics have accepted without question his commitment to the Paterian doctrine of 'Art for Art's Sake', at least in the early part of his career. This has caused misreadings of his later poetry, such as the Byzantium poems. Recently, in his introduction to a collection of essays on *The Byzantium Poems* (Columbus, Ohio: Ohio University Press, 1970), Richard Finneran accurately suggested that Yeats's view in these poems is at least partially ironic.
30 *Ibid.*, I, 249.
31 *Ibid.*
32 *Ibid.*, I, 250.
33 *Ibid.*, I, 250. Emphasis added.
34 *Letters.*, p. 198. O'Leary also regularly lent money to J. B. Yeats, the poet's father.
35 *Ibid.*, p. 263.
36 *Ibid.*
37 *Autobiographies*, p. 209.
38 *Ibid.*, p. 211.
39 *Ibid.*, p. 213.
40 *Letters.*, p. 255.
41 *Ibid.*, pp. 302, 328.
42 Yeats's attitude toward Hyde's poetry was not consistent if we may judge from "At the Abbey Theatre". (First printed in *The Irish Review* [December, 1912]; reprinted in *Responsibilities and Other Poems* [London: Macmillan, 1916]; appears in definitive edition [1956], p. 94.) The Poem's attitude is one of condescension and bitterness:

> Dear Craoibhin Aoibhin, look into our case.
> When we are high and airy hundreds say
> That if we hold that flight they'll leave the place,
> While those same hundreds mock another day
> Because we have made our art of common things,
> So bitterly, you'd dream they longed to look
> All their lives through into some drift of wings.
> You've dandled them and fed them from the book
> And know them to the bone; impart to us—

We'll keep the secret—a new trick to please.
Is there a bridle for this Proteus
That turns and changes like his draughty seas?
Or is there none, most popular of men,
But when they mock us, that we mock again?

Hyde/Craoibhin Aoibhin is father to the Protean mob which rejects the work of the Abbey—and he is mocked in return for his tricks that 'please'.

⁴³ Frayne in *Uncollected Prose* notes (I, 186) that: 'this review was included in the 1893 *The Celtic Twilight* under the title "The Four Winds of Desire", but it was omitted from the 1901 edition and never after reprinted'.
⁴⁴ See *Uncollected Prose*, I, 174.
⁴⁵ *Ibid.*, I, 292.
⁴⁶ *Autobiographies*, p. 217.
⁴⁷ *Uncollected Prose*, I, 175-182.
⁴⁸ *Ibid.*, I, 175.
⁴⁹ *Letters*, p. 321.
⁵⁰ *Autobiographies*, p. 245.
⁵¹ *Uncollected Prose*, I, 169-173.
⁵² *Ibid.*, I, 173.
⁵³ First printed in *The National Observer*, 29 July 1893; reprinted in *The Celtic Twilight* (London: Lawrence & Bullen, 1893); reprinted in *The Celtic Twilight* (London: A. H. Bullen, 1902); reprinted in *Mythologies* (London: Macmillan, 1962); appears in definitive edition (1956), p. 56.
⁵⁴ *Mythologies*, p. 5.
⁵⁵ *Uncollected Prose*, p. 173.
⁵⁶ *Mythologies*, p. 5.
⁵⁷ *Ibid.*
⁵⁸ Columcille (also called Columba and Colmcille) is an historical Irish figure known as a major saint, and copier of some 300 books. He was a prince related to both Ulster and Western Scottish royal houses. In 563 he and twelve followers went into exile on the island of Hy, later known as Iona, and created a Christian order separate from the Roman Church. The Irish influence was only defeated by the Roman cause at the Synod of Whitby in A.D. 664. See *Dictionary of Irish Writers*, comp., Brian Cleeve (Cork: Mercier, 1971), III, 31-32. Yeats used Columcille many times in his writing. At least one of the reasons this particular saint appealed to Yeats was his heretical stance; Columcille moved back toward Pagan belief in his heresy. During the 'nineties, when island solitude loomed so largely in Yeats's dreams, Columcille's example must have been congenial.
⁵⁹ *Autobiographies*, p. 207.
⁶⁰ *Ibid.* Emphasis added.
⁶¹ *Mythologies*, p. 107.
⁶² *Ibid.*, p. 109.
⁶³ *Ibid.*, p. 76.
⁶⁴ *Ibid.*, p. 7.
⁶⁵ *Ibid.*, p. 43.
⁶⁶ *Ibid.*, p. 108.
⁶⁷ *Ibid.*, p. 101.
⁶⁸ *Ibid.*, p. 102.
⁶⁹ See 'Concerning the Nearness of Heaven, Earth, and Purgatory', *Mythologies*, p. 98.
⁷⁰ *Letters*, pp. 297-298.
⁷¹ *Mythologies*, p. 80.

[72] See F. A. C. Wilson, *W. B. Yeats and Tradition* (London: Methuen, 1958); and *Yeats's Iconography* (London: Methuen, 1960).
[73] *Mythologies*, p. 11.
[74] See Chapter VIII in Moore's *Unicorn* (New York: Macmillan, 1954), for a discussion of Yeats and Spiritualism.
[75] *Mythologies*, p. 13.
[76] *Autobiographies*, p. 249.
[77] *Mythologies*, p. 15.
[78] *Ibid.*, pp. 38-39.
[79] *Autobiographies*, pp. 249-250.
[80] *Mythologies*, p. 64.
[81] *Ibid.*, pp. 81-82.
[82] *Ibid.*, p. 100.
[83] *Ibid.*
[84] *Ibid.*, pp. 138-139.

CHAPTER IV

Mythology and Rituals: The Movement through 'Hodos Chameliontos' toward Synthesis

Yeats called the section of his *Autobiographies* which deals with the closing years of the 'nineties, *Hodos Chameliontos*, or the path of the chameleon. As the title suggests, the years 1896 to 1900 were a confused period in Yeats's development. Despite what he had learned from Theosophy, Cabbalism, Blake, his beginning study of Ireland's Celtic past, and despite his growing confidence about himself, Yeats suffered from the frustration of too many ideas and no adequate way to express in his poetry the beliefs he had begun to form. Everything he studied opened new questions for him and he sought to trace his ideas to their oldest sources as a kind of proof of their validity and importance. Yeats's major task during these years would be to refine his ideas about the role of the poet, and he would finally arrive at the belief that the poet who is able to incarnate ideas from the *Anima Mundi* is a kind of semi-divine, apocalyptic figure. But as the stories of *The Secret Rose*, *Autobiographies*, and Yeats's *Memoirs* indicate, his path to this idea was twisted.

Ellmann has said that 'The world Yeats builds up in the 'nineties is . . . not really an independent world at all, but a skilful evasion, neither here nor there'.[1] If we look only at the poetry, this generalization will hold. Neither the poems of *The Rose* (1893) nor of *Wind Among the Reeds* (1899) tell us as much about Yeats as does the prose from this period. Not until *Wind Among the Reeds* does what he learned from his work on Blake and Irish folklore and mythology begin to tell in his poetry; and there his attempts to make poetry of the Irish past misfire more often than not – as they do, for example, in 'The Fiddler of Dooney':[2]

> When I play on my fiddle in Dooney,
> Folk dance like a wave of the sea;
> My cousin is priest in Kilvarnet,
> My brother in Mocharabuiee.

> I passed my brother and cousin:
> They read in their books of prayer;
> I read in my book of songs
> I bought at the Sligo fair.
>
> When we come at the end of time
> To Peter sitting in state,
> He will smile on the three old spirits,
> But call me first through the gate;
>
> For the good are always the merry,
> Save by an evil chance,
> And the merry love to fiddle,
> And the merry love to dance:
>
> And when the folk there spy me,
> They will all come up to me,
> With 'Here is the fiddler of Dooney!'
> And dance like a wave of the sea.

It will be a while before Yeats can successfully put on the mask of the Folk. Like Paddy Flynn of *The Celtic Twilight*, the fiddler of Dooney recommends merriness, but much less convincingly: his voice echoes that of the same uncertain poet who wrote:

> I am haunted by numberless islands,
>   and many a Danaan shore,
> Where Time would surely forget us,
>   and Sorrow come near us no more;
> Soon far from the rose and the lily
>   and fret of the flames would we be,
> Were we only white birds, my beloved,
>   buoyed out on the foam of the sea! [3]

The Fiddler may be an early version of Yeats's peasant fools, but because he lacks the force and irony of Tom and Crazy Jane, the fiddler appeals to the version of Ireland Yeats so hated: the Ireland of the tear and the smile.[4] Yeats the poet of the 'nineties too often pleads, wishes, and begs forgiveness, while Yeats the prose-writer questions, examines, and asserts.

It should not surprise us that Yeats's prose of the 'nineties is richer in ideas and clearer in form than the poetry, for his method of creating poems relied on beginning with prose sketches. For example, in a notebook entry of March 1926, he writes about the concept of Dreaming Back as he has discussed it in *A Vision*, explaining this time how the individual may participate and help in the process. It is as if musing over the idea of dreaming stimulates what follows on the same page, in the same pen:

MYTHOLOGY AND RITUALS: 'HODOS CHAMELIONTOS'

Topic for Poem – School Children
  The thought that life will waste them perhaps that no possible life can fulfill their own dreams or even their teachers hopes. Bring in the old thought that life prepares for what never happens.[5]

The 'old thought' here is from another important piece of his prose, *Reveries over Childhood and Youth*, which ends with the statement that

> ... when I think of all the books I have read, and the wise words I have heard spoken, and of the anxiety I have given to parents and grandparents, and of the hopes that I have had, all life weighed in the scales of my own life seems to me a preparation for something that never happens.[6]

So, the 'something that never happens', which begins as a thought in the first section of *Autobiographies*, becomes linked to musing over a concept from *A Vision*, and then leaps out as a prose fragment which will result in one of the great poems, 'Among School Children'. We have evidence from the manuscripts that the prose beginning for a poem was a common practice for Yeats. It does not mean that he arbitrarily forced ideas into poetic structures; often the resultant poem differs significantly from the prose sketch. More often yet, the poem attains a complexity not suggested by the prose as in 'Among School Children'.

On a larger scale, Yeats used prose, in essays, in tales, in *A Vision* and in his *Autobiographies*, to work through, to examine and to discover concepts he would later restate in poetry. He said that *A Vision* gave him metaphors for poetry – this was a major function of all his prose; his was primarily a discursive mind.

As before 1893, from 1893 to 1900, Yeats wrote much more prose than he did poetry. From 1893 to 1896, he was in England and Paris most of the time; during this period he continued his association with the Golden Dawn and Mathers, moved deeper into Celtic mysticism and continued to dream of an Irish Mystical Order. He published his collected *Poems* (1895), and wrote the stories for *The Secret Rose*, which was published in 1897. It is in these stories that we see Yeats examining his conception of the role of the Irish poet and groping toward a definition of the successful poet as one who is semi-divine in his ability to combine magic, mythology and poetry.

As *The Secret Rose* appears in *Mythologies*, it includes nine stories: Yeats intended three others, 'Rosa Alchemica', 'The Tables of the Law', and 'The Adoration of the Magi', to be part of the volume. However, his publisher, A. H. Bullen, published the three separately, possibly because he found their content frightening.[7] Despite Yeats's statement that all of the stories are 'after the same fashion',[8] they remain separated in all editions. While *The Celtic Twilight* compiles several folk-tales, *The Secret Rose* is his first solid attempt to use the legends in addition to the folklore of Ireland.

The first story in the collection[9] was 'founded upon an eleventh century Irish romance, and follows the original very closely. . . .'[10] 'The Crucifixion of the Outcast' is the story of Cumhal, the son of Cormac, a wandering bard in the tradition of the pagan Druids, who curses in rhyme. He seeks refuge at the abbey of the White Friars, who give him a filthy, wet place to sleep, rotten food to eat, and then attempt to dissuade him from singing his pagan songs. Cumhal refuses their attempts to christianize him, and the friars decide to crucify him. As Christ stopped three times on the way to his crucifixion, Cumhal stops three times too; each time he stops he tells his killers stories from the Celtic past (of Deirdre, Usna and others), and does magic tricks. Before his death Cumhal gives all his food to the poor who watch the execution. But when Cumhal begs the poor to 'stay outcast, . . . and keep the beasts and birds from me',[11] they are angered and leave him to be eaten by the birds and wolves. His final cry is 'Outcasts, have you all turned against the outcast?'

For Yeats, literature which lacked the 'Vision of Evil'[12] was superficial. However until 'The Crucifixion of the Outcast', Yeats had not dealt with evil in his own writings. This story is the first to consider the problem of evil and the first to treat death as something more than a fortunate escape. It sets the major themes for the whole of *The Secret Rose:* pagan versus christian Ireland, poets, magic, the place of the poet in society, and apocalypse. Cumhal's crucifixion is an intimation of a kind of second coming. The friars who derive their once revolutionary religion from the crucified Christ crucify another christological figure, this time an outcast poet who receives no more support from his fellow outcasts than the first Christ received from his followers. As Christ signalled a major shift in belief, so does Yeats's revival of the pagan past in the figure of Cumhal, a poet possessed of magic and legends, as Yeats himself was a poet who hoped to be possessed of magic and legends.

But Cumhal is not understood by his society, nor are the other poets in *The Secret Rose*. In 'Out of the Rose', an old crusader knight tells an Irish youth the romantic story of his life as he dies – a story which much resembles those of Yeats's early poetic personae. After he is dead the youth says, 'He has told me a good tale ... for there was fighting in it, but I did not understand much of it, and it is hard to remember so long a story'.[13] The tale bears almost too close an allegorical relationship to Yeats's perceptions of himself and Young Ireland. While Young Ireland will not understand the Irish past, the past full of doomed romanticism because 'it is hard to remember so long a story', Yeats will remember, and as an outcast from Catholic Ireland, he will write about it.

Part of the poet's trouble in Ireland is Christianity, but part of it he brings on himself. In 'Old Men of the Twilight', an old smuggler, Michael Bruen, is confronted by a heron who becomes 'a man that seemed of infinitely great age',[14] and who tells Michael that he and his fellow herons are poets who have been cursed by Saint Patrick. They have been cursed by the saint and have been turned into birds whose deaths will come by chance for they 'shall not be certain about anything for ever and ever'.[15] The poets had a chance to accommodate to the coming of Patrick, for the old man tells Michael:

> The Druids told us, many a time, of a new Druid Patrick; and most among them were angry with him, while a few thought his doctrine merely their own doctrine set out in new images, and were for giving him welcome; but we yawned when they spoke of him. At last they came crying that he was coming to the king's house, and fell to their dispute, but we would listen to neither party, for *we disputed concerning prosody and the relative importance of rhyme and assonance, syllable, and accent;* nor were we disturbed when they passed our door with sticks of enchantment under their arms, ... for the click of our knives writing our thoughts in Ogham delighted us.[16]

The cursed poets, like Yeats's Rhymer friends, are indecisive, care more for style than reality, will not listen to the wisdom of those who see the need to cope with reality (in this specific case they will not listen to the Druid Celts' wisdom), and ignore those in possession of the power of magic (those who pass the door with sticks of enchantment); they are damned to metamorphosis and total uncertainty. Yeats, whose 'Hopes and Fears for Irish Literature' in 1892 demonstrated his consciousness of the dangers of preoccupation with form, goes farther in 'Old Man of the Twilight'. He suggests that for poets to ignore reality, to ignore the power of magic (be it that of the Druids or of Patrick), to be fascinated by a special style (for instance, Ogham, the ancient twenty letter alphabet used on wood or stone), is to invite the doom of an inhuman shape and eternal solipsism.

This is also the subject of 'The Wisdom of the King', in which the Sidhe mix some of their blood with that of a baby king, causing him to grow feathers instead of hair. Until he comes of age, his kingdom is ruled by poets who hide the truth from him by making everyone adopt the practice of wearing feathers in his hair. The part-Sidhe king grows up a very wise man who teaches 'how little divides the false and true'.[17] But his wisdom is too much for his people to understand and eventually he finds out the truth; he leaves them, telling the poets they have sinned in their enforcement of a style which denied reality. 'Wisdom', the Sidhe-king tells his people, 'the gods have made, and no man shall live by its light, for it and the hail and the rain and the thunder follow a way that is deadly to mortal things'.[18] Yeats is close here to saying not only that style cannot conceal lies, but that total wisdom (or perhaps truth) is not knowable for man, or at least for the man or poet who would try to ignore the interpenetration of the divine/magical (Sidhe) and the human. The king being a combination of human and Sidhe, spirit and matter, possesses the power to ascertain the truth despite the efforts of the poets who have lied to him. The poets have lied to the Sidhe-king as much out of fear and misunderstanding as out of desire to protect him, and they lose his wise leadership because of their lies. The poets deny the reality of their exceptional leader and thus deny themselves the semi-divine and powerful king they might have had.

The story in *The Secret Rose* Yeats later thought contained the most of him was 'Proud Costello, Macdermot's Daughter and the Bitter Tongue'. Looking back he said:

> I had put my ideal of those years, an ideal that passed away with youth, into my description of Proud Costello: he was of those ascetics of passion who keep their hearts pure for love or for hatred, as other men for God, for Mary and for the Saints.[19]

An examination of the tale does not completely corroborate Yeats's judgment of it. 'Proud Costello' is set in medieval Ireland, unlike the tales before it which are set in pre-Christian times or immediately after Patrick's arrival, and its hero, Tumaus Costello, lives in a square tower with a winding stair – as Yeats himself would later in his own life. Costello's pride contributes to the death of his beloved Una, who joins the Sidhe and curses him; he drowns himself in despair and is buried beside the body of Una. Two ash trees planted on their graves 'wove their branches together and mingled their leaves'.[21] Costello seems not so much an ascetic of passion as an unconscious, stubborn man. The story is the one in the book which seems out of place; it begs us to read into it self-deprecation on Yeats's part, especially if we read it in the light of his own later judgment. In any case, 'Proud Costello' does stand as a denunciation of pride and a romanticized view of death and love – two attitudes characteristic of Yeats's verse during the period in which he wrote the tale.

The medieval setting of 'Proud Costello' does provide a link between the distant past of the earlier stories and the fictional present of the three final tales Yeats intended to publish in *The Secret Rose*. 'Rosa Alchemica', 'The Tables of the Law', and 'The Adoration of the Magi', are all parts of the same story; they revolve around the themes of excessive mysticism and apocalypse. In the first, the narrator has published a book, *Rosa Alchemica*, which discusses the connection between art and Alchemy. It was a 'fanciful reverie over the transmutation of life into art, and a cry of measureless desire for a world made wholly of essences'.[22] The narrator is a neurotic aesthete who notes that 'even in my most perfect moment I would be two selves, the one watching with heavy eyes the other's moment of content'. Michael Robartes is introduced in this tale as the head of an Order of the Alchemical Rose to which he wishes to initiate the narrator. The initiation rite takes place in a room with floor and ceiling painted in symbols from every variety of mysticism. Everyone in the room takes part in an unearthly, trance-like dance into which the narrator 'was swept, neither consenting nor refusing'. The dance and the dancers are attacked by a mob of angry peasants. The narrator escapes, and after ten years says:

> There are moments even now when I seem to hear those voices of exultation and lamentation, and when the indefinite world, which has but half lost its mastery over my heart and my intellect, seems about to claim a perfect mastery; but I carry the rosary about my neck and when I hear, or seem to hear them, I press it to my heart and say, 'He whose name is Legion is at our doors deceiving our intellects with subtlety and flattering our heart with beauty, and we have no trust but in Thee'; and then the war that rages within me at other times is still, and I am at peace.

'The Tables of the Law' finds the narrator questioning Owen Aherne, a Catholic who has been involved with the narrator and

Michael Robartes in a group which studied Alchemy and mysticism. Aherne is in the grip of extreme orthodox mysticism, believing that:

> ... poets and painters and musicians ... so long as they embody the beauty that is beyond the grave, these children of the Holy Spirit labour at their moments with eyes upon the shining substance on which Time has heaped the refuse of creation; for the world only exists to be a tale in the ears of the coming generations.[23]

Aherne plans to travel the world in order to 'know all accidents and destinies', and to write a secret law that will ensure that the 'Kingdom of the Holy Spirit be more widely and firmly established'. The narrator wishes to argue with Aherne but doesn't; when he confronts Aherne ten years later, Aherne tells him:

> ... since I have told you the ideas, I should tell you the extreme danger they contain, or rather the boundless wickedness they contain; but when you have heard this we must part, and part for ever, because I am lost, and must be hidden!

Aherne has lost himself – lost his soul because of his excessive preoccupation with the mystical search for complete spiritual beauty – the beauty of form alone. His fate is similar to Robartes's in 'Rose Alchemica', for the narrator believes him 'to have been driven into some distant country by the spirits whose name is Legion, and whose throne is the indefinite abyss, and whom he obeys and cannot see'.

Robartes and Aherne have been read as two sides of Yeats's personality and there is justification for this assumption, for Yeats did fear absorption into mysticism, whether of the pagan, dance-oriented variety or the orthodox, pure-style directed one. Ellmann sees Robartes and Aherne as evidence of the split he finds in Yeats's personality from 1885 to 1903,[24] the split between the active man (Robartes) and the contemplative (Aherne), but this reading over-simplifies, for it ignores the narrator in the tales. Though he is not precisely Yeats (who never wore a rosary and was never attracted to Catholicism as were many of his contemporaries), he is as much a part of Yeats's personality as are Robartes and Aherne. The narrator escapes the consequences both characters suffer as a result of their single-mindedness, just as Yeats saw the necessity of maintaining a balance between the 'asiatic fanaticism'[25] of sacrificing himself to images (Robartes) and the equally fanatic dedication to form he saw in the Rhymers

(Aherne), and wished to escape the consequences of both. The narrator in 'Rosa Alchemica' and 'The Tables of the Law' does not decide conclusively against Robartes as he does against Aherne. In both stories he is more horrified at his perception of the inverse sides of a common problem than he is decisive in his judgments on Robartes and Aherne. The nameless narrator is, in a sense, that side of Yeats which saw the problems of the Robartes and the Aherne in himself but also saw that he would have to struggle more against Robartes's problem than Aherne's. Yeats will struggle against mysticism, against the desire to say:

> Far-off, most secret, and inviolate Rose
> Enfold me in my hour of hours; where those
> Who sought thee in the Holy Sepulchre,
> Or in the wine-vat, dwell beyond the stir
> And tumult of defeated dreams; and deep
> Among pale eye-lids, heavy with the sleep
> Men have named beauty.[26]

Yeats's narrator in these stories suggests to me that he was more complex and conscious than Ellmann has indicated. Even while he writes his mystical, escapist 'rose poems', Yeats is aware of the dangers he courts. He will escape the problems of Robartes and Aherne, as his narrator escapes, but he will do it through consciousness and not through fortunate accident.

'The Adoration of the Magi' was the tale Yeats meant to end *The Secret Rose*. As the beginning story, 'The Crucifixion of the Outcast', suggests a new apocalypse, the final one indicates the event has taken place. The narrator is the same figure we have followed through 'Rosa Alchemica' and 'The Tables of the Law', though now he is wiser and dreads 'the illusion which comes of that inquietude of the veil of the Temple, which M. Mallarmé considers a characteristic of our times'.[27] Three brothers from the Aran islands come to his house to tell a tale of having been sent by the voice of the dead Michael Robartes to witness the birth of one who will change the world; they have returned from Paris where they have seen what Robartes promised. Having told their story to the narrator, they leave him to speculate:

> They may, for all I or any man can say, have been themselves Immortals: immortal demons, come to put an untrue story into my mind for some purpose I do not understand. Whatever they were, I have turned into a pathway which will lead me from them and from the Order of the Alchemical Rose.[28]

He wishes to put an old Gaelic prayer between himself and 'the demons of the air'. Again, the narrator is not precisely Yeats, but he does reflect something of Yeats's state of mind as he finished *The Secret Rose*. In the heavy, ornate prose of the last three tales, the narrator insists on his individuality in the face of highly seductive mystical systems: for example,

> I had gathered about me all gods because I believed in none, but held myself apart, individual, indissoluble, a mirror of polished steel. I looked in the triumph of this imagination at the birds of Hera, glittering in the light of the fire as though of Byzantine mosaic; and to my mind, for which symbolism was a necessity, they seemed the doorkeepers of my world, shutting out all that was not of as affluent a beauty as their own. . . .[29]

Perhaps the language is intended to reflect the complex confusions of the narrator, but the confusion and the assertion of individual indissolubility belong also to Yeats. He knew already what some of the problems with his poetry were – vagueness, sentimentality, lack of irony, escapism. He also knew how much he needed and wanted to make the Celtic past a major part of his poetry, how much he wanted to re-make Irish culture after the pattern of simplicity and unity he saw in folk-belief. Like his narrator in 'The Adoration of the Magi', Yeats wished to put a kind of old Gaelic prayer between himself and the confusion of the many gods he had gathered about him.

But, though Yeats asserts in the first nine stories that the poet is for him a semi-divine figure who by combining magic, mythology and poetry may significantly influence society, he also recognizes the dangers inherent in his position. In the first place, like Cumhal, he may be rejected by his culture and literally or metaphorically crucified. In the second place, and perhaps more importantly, he may become the victim of the mystical systems he must study, as the last three tales suggest. Yeats could never guarantee he would escape ridicule for his beliefs but he would fight the by now familiar danger of absorption into a system. As his narrator in 'Rosa Alchemica' seeks a pathway away from the immortal demons, Yeats sought a way out of the danger of absorption through conscious experimentations with magical and telepathic rituals. He plunged further into *Hodos Chameliontos* seeking a way out of his confusion and greater control over the material he studied.

To begin re-making Irish culture and to test his own beliefs, Yeats worked harder than ever on the rituals for the Irish Mystical

Order, which he wanted to establish at 'Castle Rock' on Lough Key. He wanted to

> set before Irishmen for special manual an Irish literature which, though made by many minds, would seem the work of a single mind, and turn our places of beauty or legendary association into holy symbols. I did not think this philosophy would be altogether pagan, for it was plain that its symbols must be selected from all those things that had moved men most during many mainly Christian, centuries.[30]

He worked at creating the rituals by the method Mathers had explained to him (holding symbols to his forehead and waiting for images to rise to consciousness) and found himself 'plunged without a clue into a labyrinth of images'.[31] Yeats thought he was working toward a philosophy for Ireland; in fact, he was working toward his own mythology and found himself with too many sources. The correspondences overwhelmed him and he was near collapse as he finished *The Secret Rose*. He had said in that book that 'there is no dangerous idea which does not become less dangerous when written out in sincere and careful English'.[32] Perhaps part of his problem in 1896–97 was that he knew how important 'sincere and careful' English was to the articulation of his ideas but could not yet firmly grasp and hold that style.

In the summer of 1896 Yeats went to the West of Ireland to discuss plans for the Celtic Order; it was to be an important journey even though the plans for the order never came to fruition. While there he came to know George Moore and Edward Martyn[33] (at whose castle, Tulira, he stayed for a time), who would work with him to establish an Irish theatre, but, most importantly, he met Lady Gregory. Though he did not attempt completely to understand where these three, and John Synge whom he met later in 1896 in Paris, fitted into his life as he wrote *The Trembling of the Veil*, they were to be central figures for him for the rest of his life. It was also during that summer he first visited the Aran Islands and saw for himself the strength and power of the Celtic past in the legends and the language of the islanders.

What Yeats himself chose to record as most important about that summer, however, he records in the section of *Autobiographies* entitled 'Hodos Chameliontos'. It was the time he spent with his uncle George Pollexfen, who supported him in the idea of an Irish Order and co-operated in developing the rituals through the use of telepathic magic. Though Pollexfen was a 'Unionist and Tory of the most obstinate kind, and knew nothing of Irish Literature or history',[34] he had been, like O'Leary and Yeats, devoted to Parnell. He became, in his political conservatism, stubbornness, and devotion to the people of the West of Ireland, another of Yeats's proud and lonely figures for his own mythology.

Together old Pollexfen and Yeats practiced co-ordinating their visions, inspired by the symbols Mathers had given Yeats to 'start reverie'. Yeats tells us:

> I adopted the practice of walking by the seashore while he walked on cliff or sandhill; I without speaking, would imagine the symbol, and he would notice what passed before his mind's eye, and in a short time he would practically never fail of the appropriate vision . . . gradually we found ourselves well fitted for this work, and he began to take as lively an interest as possible . . . in my plans for the Castle on the Rock.[35]

He already knew that two people could share visions inspired by the same symbolic influence but now he discovered that George Pollexfen's second-sighted servant, Mary Battle, a woman not at all connected to Cabbalism but only to the folk-beliefs of Western Ireland, shared their visions. The two men never began their work until she was upstairs in bed and yet they would hear her crying in her sleep from nightmares and in the morning would find that her dream echoed their visions.[36] Yeats gives us a significant example of this:

> One night, started by what symbol I forget, we had seen an allegorical marriage of Heaven and Earth. When Mary Battle brought in the breakfast next morning, I said, 'Well, Mary, did you dream of anything last night?' And she replied (I am quoting from an old notebook) 'indeed she had', and that it was 'a dream she would not have like to have had twice in one night'. She had dreamed that her bishop, the Catholic bishop of Sligo, had gone away 'without telling anybody', and had married 'a very high-up lady, and she not too young, either'. She had thought in her dream, 'Now all the clergy will get married, and it will be no use going to confession'. There were 'layers upon layers of flowers, many roses, all round the church'.[37]

Neither Pollexfen nor Mary Battle had the background of Yeats and his fellow Cabbalists but they could both summon images whose source Yeats was sure was not always the memory.[38] He was also sure that the visions they were experiencing were deeper than trance or dream.[39] Because of his experiments with Pollexfen and Mary Battle, combined with the work he continued to do with

MYTHOLOGY AND RITUALS: 'HODOS CHAMELIONTOS'

Mathers and the Golden Dawn students, Yeats came to see that though he 'had as yet no clear answer', he was finally

> ... face to face with the Anima Mundi described by Platonic philosophers, and more especially in modern times by Henry More, which has a memory independent of embodied individual memories, though they constantly enrich it with their images and their thought.[40]

Though he had approached formulation of the *Anima Mundi* concept many times before, almost as if by instinct, Yeats did not fully accept it until the summer of 1896. He considered at length the fact that as Mary Battle received the thoughts of his and George Pollexfen's experiments and coarsened or turned them to caricature, so too her 'folk-images' could affect his dreams. 'One night', he remembers, 'I saw between sleeping and waking a strange long bodied pair of dogs, one black and one white, that I found presently in some country tale'.[41] From this he speculated that 'the thought of the scholar or hermit . . . [may] pass into the general mind', and that 'the emotion of some woman of fashion, caught in the subtle terror of self analyzing passion, [may] pass down, with one knows not what nightmare melancholy, to Tom the Fool'.[42]

In the midst of *Hodos Chameliontos* he will not state with certainty what he was later most positive about: as he put it then,

> Seeing that a vision could divide itself in divers complementary portions, might not the thought of philosopher or poet or mathematician depend at every moment of its progress upon some complementary thought in minds perhaps at a great distance?[43]

Yeats's concept of the *Anima Mundi* will posit it as a living, vital force linking humans to all other humans, past, present, and even future; it depends upon his belief in the synchronicity of thought, as the above statement indicates.[44] What frightened him when he first approached the idea of *Anima Mundi* based on synchronicity was that unless he could know *all* of the past, how could he judge any of the present? Or, worse still, how could he communicate such ideas in his poetry? He told himself that he had not 'wilfully, nor through love of strangeness, nor love of excitement, nor because in some experimental circle',[45] taken up the ideas which now troubled him. He did it, he assured himself, because of 'unaccountable' things in his childhood and because the contemporary world ignored 'so momentous a part of human experience' as the *Anima Mundi* and the events connected to it. He asked:

Was modern civilization a conspiracy of the subconscious? Did we turn away from certain thoughts and things because the Middle Ages lived in terror of the dark, or had some seminal illusion been imposed upon us by beings greater than ourselves for an unknown purpose?

Yeats, in his fumbling and questioning in the 'nineties was not so much sceptical about the existence of *Anima Mundi*, as Ellmann and others have asserted, as he was horrified by the possibilities the idea opened and the responsibilities it entailed. If he could, by the magical practices he learned from Mathers, open himself to the 'memory of the race',[46] how could he keep separate the images; how could he distinguish the important from the trivial? He began tracing ideas back to their earliest use, searching for a 'tradition of belief older than any European Church, and founded upon the experience of the world before the modern bias'. But he found himself lost:

> ... Now image called up image in an endless procession and I could not always choose among them with any confidence; and when I did choose the image lost its intensity, or changed to some other image.

He was not to be lost to his visions as Russell and other mystics had been, but he was confused and would remain so for some time. It was to be the stage, to which he devoted so much time in the years between 1897 and 1912,[47] and direct experience with the visions and beliefs of the Irish country people, which would begin to help Yeats to clarify the problems which began to confront him in the mid-'nineties.

Yeats spent the summer of 1897 at Coole Park, Lady Gregory's estate; for many summers to come he was to repeat this visit until Coole became for him the home he never had with his parents. As John O'Leary functioned in the role of substitute father, Augusta Gregory could be considered another mother for Yeats. In May of 1897 we find among Yeats's letters the first to O'Leary which does not ask for money or excuse non-payment of it. Lady Gregory supplanted O'Leary as money-lender and out-did him as caretaker for the confused and physically ill Yeats. She forced him to rest, to write, and to eat. Almost as a form of therapy for his debilitating depressions, she took him out from cottage to cottage 'to gather folk-belief, tales of the faeries, and the like. . . .'[48] He had begun this project the summer before during his visit to the Aran Islands with his uncle, but it was Lady Gregory who directed him back to

MYTHOLOGY AND RITUALS: 'HODOS CHAMELIONTOS'

it and kept him at it for several summers. Before, he had sought and found his information primarily in the written lore of Ireland, in translations and histories; now he talked with the people themselves. The effect was to be significant because, like Mary Battle, the people of the Western countryside spoke in an idiom both simple and passionate. Yeats later described it as being influenced by Gaelic and retaining the Seventeenth-century English idiom;[49] he was to try for years to translate this idiom into his own poetry.

Though Lady Gregory is most remembered for her work with the Irish theatre, it was the work in folk-lore she did with Yeats which would most directly influence his philosophy and his poetry. The ideas he gathered with her appeared first and most crudely in the drama he wrote before 1912. Yeats used the stage in these years to try out his ideas for poetry in a dramatic setting. He had, of course, other motives behind his early drama, mainly cultural and political ones. He decided he would never reach a large enough audience with his poetry to influence the kind of change he wanted in Ireland; he hoped in the beginning of his work with the Irish Theatre to direct Ireland to the unity of culture he saw as essential to its future, and perhaps to his own. In 1897–98 he made his last attempts to mediate between the London Irish Nationalists and the Dublin Fenians by accepting the chairmanship of the '98 Commemoration Association of Great Britain.

The supposed object of the Dublin and London groups was the erection of a memorial to Wolfe Tone, who had been martyred for his attempted revolt in 1798 and had become one of the patron saints of the Irish revolutionary movement. Quarrels broke out between the Dublin and London Nationalists over the issue of a political murder. Their differences were deep and lasting, for the younger Dublin group favoured a complete break with England by violent means if necessary and the London group would have settled for a Parnellite Union. Yeats's efforts at mediation over the memorial were to be successful but anti-climatic, for in 1897, the year of Victoria's Jubilee, riots broke out in Dublin which were the beginning of the final split between leftists and Parnellites. Yeats had 'dreaded some wild Fenian movement',[50] and had planned what he later described as a 'premature impossible peace between those two devouring heads'. He took his politics from the conservative O'Leary and found himself initially benumbed by the spectre of violence:

> ... I hear a sound of breaking glass, the crowd has begun to stone the windows of the decorated houses, [decorated for

Victoria's jubilee] and when I try to speak that I may restore order, I discover that I have lost my voice. . . . I can only whisper and gesticulate, and as I am thus freed of responsibility, I share the emotion of the crowd, and perhaps even feel as they feel when the glass crashes. Maud Gonne has a look of exultation as she walks with her laughing head thrown back.[51]

Yeats's loss of his voice was both a relief for the moment and significant for the future. 'Perhaps', he says, he felt the emotion of the crowd; surely Maude Gonne felt it and her exultation at the violence remained with Yeats the rest of his life. Yeats was, as always, not able to freely hate the British, nor to freely love the violence. Later that same night Connolly led a procession which threw a coffin marked 'British Empire' into the Liffey; fights between police and demonstrators left several dead and two hundred wounded. When Yeats read of it in the morning he said, 'I count the links in the chain of responsibility, run them across my fingers, and wonder if any link there is from my workshop'.[52] Conor Cruise O'Brien scornfully dismisses any responsibility on Yeats's part, judging him too Anglo-Irish to have had any influence.[53] What is important is not whether Yeats had any responsibility but that he believed – and always would – that something he wrote *might* influence action. It is difficult to see anything he wrote before 1897 that might have led to revolutionary violence, but, ambivalent as is his attitude toward the violence, Yeats wanted his poetry to be that powerful.

After 1897–98, Yeats turned away from active revolutionary politics and toward the theatre. When he lectured in America in 1904 on Robert Emmet, he wrote to Lady Gregory:

I am dreadfully busy over my Emmet lecture, which is a frightful nuisance. It is indeed, as you say, a sword dance, and I must give it every moment. I had no idea until I started on it how completely I have thought myself out of the whole stream of traditional Irish feeling on such subjects. I am just as strenuous a Nationalist as ever, but I have got to express these things differently.[54]

Yeats would always be a Nationalist and eventually a Senator for the Free State, but the lessons of the libraries scheme and the violence of 1897–98 taught him that he had no place with the Connollys, Pearses and MacBrides. He would, as he said himself, have to express his Nationalist feelings differently, in a most individual poetry.

In the second half of the 'nineties, in addition to continuing his

MYTHOLOGY AND RITUALS: 'HODOS CHAMELIONTOS'

connections with Mathers and the Cabbalists, working to develop the Irish Mystical Order, gathering Irish Folk-lore, starting the Irish Theatre and ending his active participation in revolutionary politics, Yeats continued his association wth the Rhymers group, actively sorting his own identity as poet in relation to the poets he saw around him. As Yeats retraces the 'nineties in 'The Tragic Generation', section four of *The Trembling of the Veil*, he amplifies themes he suggested in the previous sections of *Autobiographies:* his definition of art, his perceptions of personalities, the place of magic and Ireland in his life. We see Yeats grow more complex, more conscious of history and alternately certain and confused as we move through his retracing of the formative period in his experience. In 'The Tragic Generation', what emerges most significantly as part of the base of Yeats's own mythology is his evaluative memories of the people around him – Wilde, Shaw, Henley, Beardsley, Johnson, Dowson, William Sharpe/Fiona Macleod, Verlaine, and Synge. He compares and contrasts these figures with each other and then with himself.[55] This was a favourite tactic of Yeats, especially during the 'nineties, as we may observe from the fictional characters, John Sherman and William Howard, in the short romance, *John Sherman*. Sherman and Howard are more clearly the active man and the contemplative man, played off against each other as possible sides of Yeats's own character than are Robartes and Aherne.[56]

As Yeats employed this technique in fiction in the 'nineties, he re-uses it in reconstructing his memories of the real characters from that same period. For example, set against the decadence of London, we see Shaw through Yeats's eyes:

> ... I listened to *Arms and the Man* with admiration and with hatred. It seemed to me inorganic, logical straightness and not the crooked road of life, yet I stood aghast before its energy.... Shaw was right to claim Samuel Butler for his master, for Butler was the first Englishman to make the discovery that it is possible to write with great effect without music, without style, ... to eliminate from the mind all emotional implication and to prefer plain water to every vintage. ... Presently I had a nightmare that I was haunted by a sewing machine, that clicked and shone, but the incredible thing was that the machine smiled, smiled perpetually.[57]

Shaw becomes the first of Yeats's examples of the objective man – the man who like a sewing machine clicks and shines and smiles perpetually. While his attitude toward Shaw seems to contain ambivalence, we can only understand Yeats's full evaluation when we look also at Wilde from his perspective. 'I might have known that Wilde's fantasy had taken some tragic turn, and that he was meditating upon possible disaster', Yeats says, '. . . had he not called insincerity "a mere multiplication of the personality. . . ."'[58] Understanding Wilde's suicidal suit against Lord Queensbury better than most critics have since his time, Yeats saw that Wilde's 'elaborate playing with tragedy, was an attempt to escape from an emotion by its exaggeration'.[59] Shaw and Wilde, in Yeats's *Autobiographies*, become two halves of one unity, as Robartes and Aherne exist in mirror-like relation to each other:

> Shaw and Wilde, had no catastrophe come, would have long divided the stage between them, though they were most unlike – for Wilde believed himself to value nothing but words in their emotional associations, and he had turned his style to a parade as though it were his show, and he Lord Mayor.[60]

Wilde in his intense subjectivity was completely out of his time, even declaring himself (in advance of Eliot) a monarchist in politics. But Shaw who carried his 'street-corner Socialist eloquence on to the stage', had, Yeats decides, 'no true quarrel with his time'. He was 'quite content to exchange Narcissus and his Pool for the signal-box at a railway junction, where goods and travellers pass perpetually upon their logical glittering road'.[61]

In analysing Shaw and Wilde, Yeats has an interest beyond the mere recording of his opinions. As he wrote this section of his *Autobiographies*, he worked on material for the 'Twenty-Eight Incarnations' section of *A Vision*, and if we read closely what he says about history and personality in 'The Tragic Generation', that section of *A Vision* becomes much clearer.[62] Yeats concisely states his theory of history in 'The Tragic Generation', and in many places throughout his later work:

> Somewhere about 1450, though later in some parts of Europe by a hundred years or so, and in some earlier, men attained to personality in great numbers, 'Unity of Being', and as men so fashioned held places of power, their nations had it too, prince and ploughman sharing that thought and feeling.[63]

The divided personalities Yeats saw around him were evidence, he thought, of how far the world had moved from that perfect state he so hoped to re-create in his early years. If he was to integrate his own personality in an age which was itself *Hodos Chameliontos*, he would have to understand not only the time when

Unity of Culture had been possible, but also his own time; for Yeats, personalities were history, were time itself.

It was in remembering the people around him in the 'nineties that Yeats formed his ideas of personality and history; of Will and Mask; of subjective and objective. Simultaneously he made a pattern of his life and friends, and proposed a pattern for all history and all humans. Yeats's description of Shaw and Wilde suggests much, but his treatment of Johnson and Dowson, whom he knew better, reveals even more about himself and his theories.

Lionel Johnson was a tiny, insomniac recluse, devoted to his library and his Catholicism. As Yeats studied the Cabbala, Johnson studied Newman and the Church fathers. Looking back, Yeats saw that 'in some half-conscious part of him', Johnson 'desired the world he had renounced'.[64] When he first knew him, though, Johnson seemed his complete opposite – an orthodox, Catholic scholar. He records that,

> ... not till some time in 1895 did I think he could ever drink too much for his sobriety – though what he drank would certainly be too much for that of most of the men whom I knew – I no more doubted his self-control, ... than I doubted his memories of Cardinal Newman. The discovery that he did was a great shock to me and, I think, altered my general view of the world.[65]

Johnson contemplated his future degradation with pleasure, causing Yeats to wonder if 'the austerity, the melancholy of his thoughts, that spiritual ecstasy which he touched at times', heightened 'not only the Vision of Evil, but its fascination'.[66] As he judged Emerson and Whitman deficient in their lack of a vision of evil, he judged Johnson to be doomed by an excess of it: the celibate Catholic would write *The Dark Angel,* and to Yeats it seemed that within one personality, opposites reached for each other. The more sterile Johnson's life appeared, the darker and more sensual his vision.

While Johnson was a scholarly, celibate alcoholic who wrote darkly sensual poetry, Dowson was an alcoholic satyr whose poetry, Yeats said, 'shows how sincerely he felt the fascination of religion, but his religion had certainly no dogmatic outline, being but a desire for a condition of virginal ecstasy'.[67] Dowson's personality was the opposite of Johnson's in outward aspect; his vision was opposite too, reaching for purity where Johnson's reached for sensuality. Yeats balanced both men against each other and both against himself. He would not make the mistakes of Shaw and Wilde, nor of Johnson and Dowson – their tragedy was in being unconscious of what worked beneath the surface of their minds. Yeats, examining them, examines himself, forever cautioning himself, as did his narrator in the final three *Secret Rose* tales, against excess of any kind:

> They had taught me that violent energy, which is like a fire of straw, consumes in a few minutes the nervous vitality, and is useless in the arts. Our fire must burn slowly, and we must constantly turn away to think, constantly analyse what we have done, be content even to have little life outside our work, to show, perhaps, to other men, as little as the watch-mender shows, his magnifying glass caught in his screwed-up eye. Only then do we learn to conserve our vitality, to keep our mind enough under control to make our technique sufficiently flexible for expression of the emotions of life as they arise.[68]

The whole pattern of Yeats's work indicates how firmly he did believe in the necessity constantly to re-think, re-analyse everything he had done; he may indeed have learned this from his experience in the 'nineties. But his further corollary, that the artist must be 'content to have little life outside' his work, was one of the propositions he would analyse again and again. In 1931, he would write:

> The intellect of man is forced to choose
> Perfection of the life, or of the work,
> And if it take the second must refuse
> A heavenly mansion, raging in the dark.
> When all that story's finished, what's the news?
> In luck or out the toil has left its mark:
> That old perplexity an empty purse,
> Or the day's vanity, the night's remorse.[69]

When this octave appeared in *The Winding Stair* collection, Yeats titled it 'The Choice'; it was a choice he could never make with finality. He was aware that choosing perfection of the work meant to rage in the dark, having refused the 'heavenly mansion' of full involvement in life. But as the final couplet indicates, choice of either absolute could mean poverty, vanity, and remorse. Instead of choosing, Yeats reinforces the strength of his oscillation.

What Yeats did learn from the men of the 'nineties he would repeat to himself again and again: he would struggle against extremism of any kind, constantly thinking and analysing himself, his work, his sources, his magic. He would do so because, as he put it:

MYTHOLOGY AND RITUALS: 'HODOS CHAMELIONTOS'

Does not all art come when a nature, that never ceases to judge itself, exhausts personal emotion in action or desire so completely that something impersonal, something that has nothing to do with action or desire, suddenly starts into its place, something which is as unforeseen, as completely organized, even as unique, as the images that pass before the mind between sleeping and waking?[70]

Central to the core of Yeats's beliefs, this statement puts as a rhetorical question an idea he was fully to elaborate in the twentieth century. Art cannot emerge from a non-conscious personality – only from never-ceasing self-judgment which leads to the twilight state from whence the images of all art proceed.

How important consciousness is to Yeats's definition of the twilight state where hypnogogic vision is possible becomes evident in the final pages of 'The Tragic Generation'. Though he was part of this generation, he was always more an observer than a participant. He sums up what he has learned of the dangers of unconscious excess and mysticism in his cryptic reference to an evening he spent in Paris with the followers of Saint-Martin. The experience is detailed in 'Discoveries', which he most certainly consulted to refresh his own memories of the end of the century. He had taken hashish and remembers his reactions:

> ... I felt suddenly that a cloud I was looking at floated in an immense space, and for an instant my being rushed out, as it seemed, into that space with ecstasy. I was myself again immediately, but the poet [who had given him the hashish] was wholly above himself, and presently he pointed to one of the street-lamps now brightening in the fading twilight, and cried at the top of his voice, 'Why do you look at me with your great eye'?[71]

Yeats says, 'I never forgot myself, never rose above myself for more than a moment, and was even able to feel the absurdity of that gaiety'[72] which the others with him seemed to experience. He was not able completely to lose consciousness under the influence of hashish any more than he was able to follow the mysticism of Russell, or the excesses of politics, or the 'nervous rhythms'[73] of the Rhymers. To constrict or to lose consciousness through politics, aestheticism, mysticism, or drugs would be disastrous to his art. 'Alas', he said, 'that the hangman's rope should be own brother to that Indian happiness that keeps alone, were it not for some stray cactus, mother of as many dreams, immemorial impartiality'.[74] Drugs, like any other excess, are for Yeats the same as death; hashish and peyote are escapes not available to him. He will never enjoy 'immemorial impartiality', as he was never fully part of the tragic generation.

Though Yeats would slip again into *hodos chameliontos* before reaching his mature poetic achievement, the end of his second section of *Autobiographies*, 'The Stirring of the Bones', finds him affirming consciousness and magic as the sources of inspiration for him. He had ended 'The Tragic Generation' on the apocalyptic note carried over from *The Secret Rose*, saying,

> After Stéphane Mallarmé, after Paul Verlaine, after Gustave Moreau, after Puvis de Chavannes, after our own verse [the Rhymers], after all our subtle colour and nervous rhythm, after the faint mixed tints of Condor, what more is possible? After us the Savage God.[75]

But, in 'The Stirring of the Bones', Yeats suggests something may survive among the bones of the *fin-de-siècle* decadence. He had found Coole and Lady Gregory; together with John Synge they would form the nucleus of the Abbey Theatre, a project which had begun to take over his interest as the plans for the Irish Mystical Order faltered. And, it was at Coole he tells us, that 'the first few simple thoughts that now, grown complex through their contact with other thoughts, explain the world, came to me from beyond my own mind'.[76]

He had been practicing meditations which affected his sleep so that he began having 'dreams that differed from ordinary dreams in seeming to take place amid brilliant light, and by their invariable coherence, and certain half-dreams . . . between sleep and waking'.[77] One of these brilliantly lit dreams (again hypnogogic by his description) allowed him to make the connection for himself between Christianity and Pagan Ireland that he had seen made by the country-people in their stories. He describes it:

> I was crossing a little stream near Inchy Wood and actually in the middle of a stride from bank to bank, when an emotion never experienced before swept down upon me. I said, 'That is what the devout Christian feels, that is how he surrenders his will to the will of God'. I felt an extreme surprise, for my whole imagination was preoccupied with the Pagan mythology of ancient Ireland; I was marking in red ink, upon a large map, every sacred mountain.[78]

Before, Yeats had used the symbols Mathers gave him to induce reverie, to penetrate his own unconscious mind, and thus to connect to the *Anima Mundi*. Now, the map of ancient Ireland has become the meditative symbol, inducing his metaphoric, brilliantly lit, hypnogogic dream. What had been an abstract, intellectualized matter for him – the Folk-lore and mythology of ancient Ireland – he now internalized. As he saw the peasants connect Catholicism with their ancient Pagan beliefs, he was finally able, with the help of the method taught him by Mathers, to feel, rather than merely see, the connection between the Celtic past and other central mythologies, such as Christianity.

The years from 1896 to 1900 were full and confusing for Yeats. The stories of *The Secret Rose* reflect his growing belief in the power of the poet who could combine in his poetry the magical and the human. But they also indicate the fear of absorption Yeats felt as a result of the occult studies in which he engaged. Yeats tested his ideas and beliefs in Cabbalistic rituals he conducted with his uncle, George Pollexfen, and finally accepted the concept he would later call the *Anima Mundi*. But he had yet to gain the courage necessary to state publicly his beliefs in magic and the *Anima Mundi*, nor did he know how to write about his discoveries. He made his last attempts to influence the politics of pre-revolutionary Ireland and found that his was not to be a political contribution to his country. Yeats would leave it to the MacBrides and the Connollys to make a revolution; he would write about it.

Everywhere he looked at the end of the nineteenth century, Yeats saw divided men, caught in the nets of total absorption in Catholicism, alcohol, promiscuity, and mysticism. But by the end of the 'nineties, Yeats knew what would not only save him from absorption but also make him a great poet: the conscious use of rituals which would induce visions and help him to incarnate ideas from the *Anima Mundi*. His previously unpublished *Memoirs* affirms the certainty he felt in the midst of the confusion of the *fin-de-siècle*. He wrote of one of his hypnogogic experiences:

> I awoke enough to know that I lay in bed and had the familiar objects round, but to hear a strange voice speaking through my lips: 'We make an image of him who sleeps, and we call it Emmanuel'.[79]

Yeats was terrified at the possibilities the concept of the *Anima Mundi* opened for him, but through the rituals of poetry and magic, and through the use of the Celtic past, he began to find his confidence again. His rituals for magic and poetry would work because they helped him to incarnate what was part of the unconscious memory we all share. Because he could do this he began to believe in himself as an 'Emmanuel' figure, a semi-divine poet. As his dream indicates, at the end of the 'nineties, Yeats was in the middle of crossing the stream which divided the centuries; he crossed successfully. He had begun to make a part of himself the Celtic past which magic opened to him. Though his poetry does not immediately show it, at his best, Yeats would feel, experience for himself, all of his subject matter, which he would gather from the Ireland of his mind.

NOTES

[1] Richard Ellmann, *Yeats, The Man and the Masks* (London: Faber and Faber, 1949), p. 165.

[2] First printed in *The Bookman*, December 1892; reprinted in *The Second Book of the Rhymers' Club* (London: Elkin Matthews, 1894); reprinted in *The Wind Among the Reeds* (London: Elkin Matthews, 1899); reprinted in *The Collected Works* (1908); appears in definitive edition (1956), p. 71. The place names, Dooney, Kilvarnet, and Mocharabuiee, ring of stage-Irish and contribute to the saccharine effect of this poem. Yeats was troubled by his choice too, adding in 1922 a note explaining that Mocharabuiee is pronounced as if spelt 'Mockrabwee'. In his later poetry he would avoid such terms with care.

[3] First printed in *The National Observer*, 7 May 1892; reprinted in *The Countess Kathleen and Various Legends and Lyrics* (London: T. Fisher Unwin, 1892); reprinted in *Poems* (1895); appears in definitive edition (1956), p. 41. The connection between 'The White Birds', and 'The Fiddler of Dooney' becomes clearer when we note that they were composd within months of each other. Although Yeats often withheld poems for years after composition, it seems strange that he chose to end *The Wind Among the Reeds* with a poem so representative of earlier and weaker work.

[4] Yeats's hatred of Irish sentimentality is easily documented, making it ironic that so much of his own early poetry is marked by the same hackneyed tone.

[5] National Library of Ireland MS. 13576. Parkinson in *The Later Poetry*, pp. 92-93 uses this prose sketch but does not link it to *Reveries*.

[6] W. B. Yeats, *Autobiographies* (London: Macmillan, 1966), p. 106; Chapter I this study, p. 18.

[7] W. B. Yeats, *Letters*, ed. Allan Wade (London: Hart-Davies, 1954), p. 280. Hereafter referred to as *Letters*.

[8] *Letters*, p. 266; a forthcoming edition will include these three tales as part of *The Secret Rose* for the first time.

[9] W. B. Yeats, *Mythologies* (London: Macmillan, 1962), pp. 147-156. Hereafter referred to as *Mythologies*.

[10] *Letters*, p. 285; in defence of 'The Crucifixion of the Outcast', Yeats cites the eleventh century legend and Giraldus Cambrensis as sources—surely this Giraldus is the source for the Giraldus of *A Vision*. He also states, interestingly, that 'history was no part of my purpose' in writing the tale. It was an effort to bring the past into the present through symbolism.

MYTHOLOGY AND RITUALS: 'HODOS CHAMELIONTOS'

[11] *Mythologies*, p. 156.
[12] *Autobiographies*, p. 246; here Yeats refers to Whitman and Emerson as 'writers who have begun to seem superficial precisely because they lack the Vision of Evil'.
[13] *Mythologies*, p. 164.
[14] *Ibid.*, p. 192.
[15] *Ibid.*, p. 195.
[16] *Ibid.*, pp. 193-194. Emphasis added.
[17] *Ibid.*, p. 170.
[18] *Mythologies*, p. 170.
[19] *Autobiographies*, p. 334.
[20] *Mythologies*, p. 197; Yeats emphasizes the medieval setting by mentioning the French and Spanish influence in Western Ireland (especially Galway) which is historically accurate.
[21] *Mythologies*, p. 210.
[22] *Ibid.*, pp. 267-292.
[23] *Ibid.*, pp. 300-307.
[24] *Man and Masks*, pp. 86-88.
[25] *Autobiographies*, p. 237.
[26] *Mythologies*, p. 145; first printed in *The Countess Kathleen and Various Legends and Lyrics* (London: T. Fisher Unwin, 1892); reprinted in *Poems* (1895); appears in definitive edition (1956), p. 67.
[27] *Mythologies*, p. 309. Yeats of course called the second section of his autobiographies *The Trembling of the Veil*.
[28] *Ibid.*, p. 315.
[29] *Mythologies*, p. 269.
[30] *Autobiographies*, p. 254.
[31] *Ibid.*, p. 255.
[32] *Mythologies*, p. 309.
[33] Yeats discusses Moore, Martyn, Lady Gregory, and Synge at further length in the 'Dramatis Personae' section of *Autobiographies*.
[34] *Autobiographies*, p. 255.
[35] *Ibid.*, pp. 258-259.
[36] *Ibid.*, p. 260.
[37] *Ibid.*, pp. 259-260.
[38] *Ibid.*, p. 261.
[39] *Ibid.*, p. 262.
[40] *Ibid.*
[41] *Ibid.*, pp. 267-268.
[42] *Ibid.*, p. 262.
[43] *Ibid.*, p. 263.
[44] See C. G. Jung, *Memories, Dreams, Reflections*, ed., Aniela Jaffe, trans., Richard and Clara Winston (New York: Alfred A. Knopf, Inc., 1961), p. 400. Jung says, 'I chose this term because the simultaneous occurrence of two meaningfully but not causally connected events seemed to me an essential criterion. I am therefore using the general concept of synchronicity in the special sense of a coincidence in time of two or more causally unrelated events which have the same or similar meaning, in contrast to "synchronism", which simply means the simultaneous occurrence of two events'. Jung, like Yeats, was speaking specifically of similar thoughts, dreams, and visions. That the two men should have discussed the concept so similarly with no causal connection between them, is another evidence of Synchronicity.

[45] *Autobiographies*, pp. 263-264.
[46] *Ibid.*, pp. 267-270.
[47] Yeats's drama is yet to be adequately assessed, but it is not within the scope of this study to include a consideration of it.
[48] *Autobiographies*, p. 377.
[49] *Ibid.*, p. 560.
[50] *Ibid.*, pp. 362-363.
[51] *Ibid.*, pp. 367-368.
[52] *Ibid.*
[53] See Conor Cruise O'Brien, 'Passion and Cunning: The Politics of W. B. Yeats', in *In Excited Reverie*, eds., A. N. Jeffares and K. G. W. Cross (London: Macmillan, 1965), pp. 207-208.
[54] *Letters*, p. 432.
[55] W. B. Yeats's *John Sherman* (London: T. Fisher Unwin, 1891); Yeats finished the book in 1888.
[56] In a preface to *John Sherman* in the *Collected Works* (London: A. H. Bullen, 1908), Yeats stresses the astrological oppositions behind his conception of Sherman-Howard.
[57] *Autobiographies*, p. 283.
[58] *Ibid.*, p. 285.
[59] *Autobiographies*, p. 287.
[60] *Ibid.*, p. 284.
[61] *Ibid.*, p. 294.
[62] I do not mean to suggest that *A Vision* is an inessential work, but it is not radically different from Yeats's ideas as we see them in *Autobiographies*.
[63] *Autobiographies*, p. 291.
[64] *Ibid.*, p. 305.
[65] *Ibid.*, p. 308. It was shortly after his experience with Johnson that Yeats wrote 'The Crucifixion of the Outcast', the first of his works to treat evil as a major theme.
[66] *Ibid.*, p. 310. Johnson is a possible model for Owen Aherne.
[67] *Ibid.*, p. 311.
[68] *Ibid.*, p. 318. See also 'In Memory of Major Robert Gregory', stanza XI:

> Some burn damp faggots, others may consume
> The entire combustible world in one small room
> As though dried straw, and if we turn about
> The bare chimney is gone black out
> Because the work had finished in that flare.

[69] First printed in *Words for Music Perhaps and Other Poems* (Dublin: Cuala Press, 1932); appears in National Library of Ireland MS. 13590, 1932 as untitled octave excised from MS. of 'Coole, 1931'; appears in definitive edition (1956), p. 242.
[70] *Autobiographies*, p. 332.
[71] W. B. Yeats, *Essays and Introductions* (London: Macmillan, 1961), p. 281.
[72] *Ibid.*, p. 282.
[73] *Autobiographies*, p. 369.
[74] *Essays and Introductions*, p. 283.
[75] *Autobiographies*, p. 349.
[76] *Ibid.*, p. 378.
[77] *Ibid.*

[78] *Autobiographies*, p. 378. Yeats had described this experience more fully in a 1902 addition to *The Celtic Twilight*, entitled 'A Voice'. There he identified the emotion as 'the root of Christian Mysticism'; the voice said 'No human soul is like any other human soul, and therefore the love of God for any human soul is infinite, for no other soul can satisfy the same need in God'. Clearly Yeats thought this work with Celtic mythology individuated and saved him from the fate of 'The Tragic Generation'.

[79] W. B. Yeats, *Memoirs*, ed., Denis Donoghue (New York: Macmillan, 1972), p. 126. The dream was published in a slightly different version in *A Vision* (New York: Macmillan, 1962), p. 233 n.

CHAPTER V

Magic and Poetry: The Path from Assertion of Belief to Confrontation of the Anti-Self and the Beginnings of Responsibility

Part I

The end of the nineteenth century was a period in which the confusion we find reflected in Yeats's prose and verse was rampant. The apocalypticism of his *The Secret Rose* tales and the Christological implications of Yeats's dream that he was an 'Emmanuel' figure were also reflections of a general end-of-the-century mood. Throughout the nineteenth century various forms of millenialism had flourished on both sides of the Atlantic,[1] perhaps partially the result of the approach of the last one hundred years of what most Westerners believed to be a one thousand year era. If apocalypticism defines the general *fin-de-siècle* mood, then Yeats's place in his time was made even more difficult. He lived in an Ireland which regularly promised revolution, and among poets who consciously believed themselves in revolt against the immediate past and in the vanguard of their own apocalyptically pure movement in poetry. But Yeats had begun to distance himself from the large events at the end of the century, and, as he later remembered the time, it signalled a change. 'The Rhymers had begun to break up in tragedy. . . . I think that perhaps our form of lyric, our insistence upon emotion which has no relation to any public interest, gathered together overwrought, unstable men';[2] he says, reinforcing all that he wrote in *The Secret Rose*.

But he will insist publicly that there was more to the tragic ends of so many of his friends and that he cannot fully explain what happened. In his 1936 introduction to the *Oxford Book of*

Modern Verse he underplays all the tragedy and apocalypticism of the time in an ironic description:

> Poets said to one another over their black coffee – a recently imported fashion – 'We must purify poetry of all that is not poetry. . . .' Poetry was a tradition like religion and liable to corruption, and it seemed that they could best restore it by writing lyrics technically perfect, their emotion pitched high, and as Pater offered instead of moral earnestness life lived as a 'pure gem-like flame' all accepted him for master. But every light has its shadow; we tumble out of one pickle into another, the 'pure gem-like flame' was an insufficient motive. . . . Then in 1900 everybody got down off his stilts; henceforth nobody drank absinthe with his black coffee; nobody went mad; nobody commited suicide; nobody joined the Catholic Church; or if they did I have forgotten.[3]

What he saw as 'a facile charm, a too soft simplicity'[4] in his own work before 1900 was present in most of the poetry of the period. He had summed up the Rhymers' problems and his own before the 1936 introduction; in the 1915 'The Scholars',[5] which was probably composed in 1912-13, he writes:

> Bald heads forgetful of their sins,
> Old, learned, respectable bald heads
> Edit and annotate the lines
> That young men, tossing on their beds,
> Rhymed out in love's despair
> To flatter Beauty's ignorant ear.
>
> All shuffle there; all cough in ink;
> All wear the carpet with their shoes;
> All think what other people think;
> All know the man their neighbour knows.

In this poem, one of Yeats's often misunderstood works, he clearly dismisses the efforts not only of a certain kind of scholar (the one who merely edits and annotates), but also of a certain kind of poet, the kind of poet he and his friends in the Rhymers' Club had been. The most obvious link to the Rhymers is in the closing couplet, 'Lord, what would they say/Did their Catullus walk that way?' (In the original version the question mark was an exclamation point – Yeats probably changed the punctuation to reinforce the rhetorical question.) Catullus, as we learn from the *Autobiographies,* and later from the introduction to the *Oxford Book of Modern Verse,* was a favourite of the Rhymers, but the Roman poet shared little with sterile scholars or unoriginal young poets. He admired and used Alexandrine forms in his work[6] but let no tradition dominate him. Developing his own voice, he influenced such writers as Horace and Virgil. Yeats's irony in the closing couplet supports his condemnation, especially of the poets, for he never mentions Catullus in any other connection but the Rhymers.

Looking back at the previous ten lines of the poem, we can see his punctuation and diction taking on key importance, as it will do in most of his later poetry. As he connects sterile scholarship with sterile poetry in his mind, so he connects the 'Old, learned, respectable bald heads' with the young men who rhyme out of despair, by making the first stanza one sentence. The first three lines concern the scholars, the second three the poets; syntactically, as well as literally, the poets and scholars depend upon each other for their meaning. In the second stanza, 'all', as in 'All shuffle there', introduces five interdependent sentences. 'All' refers to all of the scholars and all of the poets in the first stanza; all share the same problems of isolation, sterility, hopelessness, and perhaps the two worst sins Yeats could imagine, unoriginality and despair. 'The Scholars' was a title added to the poem after composition, deflecting our attention from his central target – the poetry of the Rhymers and by implication his own work before 1900.[7]

The attitudes Yeats expresses in the 1936 introduction and in 'The Scholars', consolidate the discomfort he felt throughout the 'nineties about the Rhymers and about his own work, but 1900 marks a definite shift in his attitudes and in his work. This change is often dated to 1902,[8] the year which begins a six-year period Yeats does not discuss in any of his autobiographical materials, and the point at which he ceased for nearly eight years to produce poetry: only one lyric dates from this time. From his letters, essays, and plays, which trace the direction of his concerns, we can see that the break with his past began in 1900.[9]

In an unpublished paper, George Harper[10] cites 1900 as the year Yeats remembered as 'the most difficult' of his life. With much documentation from unpublished material, Harper reasonably suggests that the difficulty stemmed from troubles with the Golden Dawn. MacGregor Mathers had become increasingly troublesome (in fact, evidence indicates increasing schizophrenia), and Yeats decided to put him out of the order. Mathers sent an envoy to protest the expulsion, Aleister Crowley, whom Yeats judged 'a quite unspeakable person'. He continued, writing to Lady Gregory, 'He is I believe seeking vengeance for our refusal to initiate him. We did not admit him because we did not think a mystical society was intended to be a reformatory'. Having successfully expelled Mathers and repulsed the unspeakable 'mad person', Crowley, Yeats seems to have headed the order for a short time. He wrote, 'At last we have got a perfectly honest order, with no false mystery and no mystagogues of any kind. Everybody is working, as I have never seen them work. . . .'[12] Clouded as the history of Yeats's trouble with Mathers and Crowley is, it took place during a significant time in his development and demands notice.[13] The 'nineties were not so much a skilful evasion, as Ellmann suggests, as they were a seed time; 1900 marks the beginning of a conscious effort on Yeats's part to sift from his life, from his magic, his philosophy, and his poetry all that was vague and imprecise. He began to make distinctions, to define and to synthesize as he had not been able to previously. In the same letter in which he describes the successful removal of Mathers and Crowley, Yeats speaks interestingly on poetry, imagination and fantasy:

> To write of a material object being 'fiery footed' is almost always to write from the phantasy rather than the imagination. The imaginative deals with spiritual things symbolised by natural things – with gods and not matter. The phantasy has its place in poetry but it has a subordinate place. . . . I would myself avoid it in poetry for the same reason that I would avoid 'haunted' and because of vague forms, pictures, scenes, etc., are rather a modern idea of the poetic and I would not want to call up a modern kind of picture. I avoid every kind of word that seems to me either 'poetical' or 'modern' and above all I avoid suggesting the ghostly (the vague) idea about a god, for it is a modern conception. *All ancient vision was definite and precise.*[14]

Though Yeats's own poetry up to 1900 would hardly bear scrutiny for proof of his unswerving avoidance of the vague and shadowy, he strongly wishes that from this point forward he will express his visions as did the ancients, definitely and precisely. As he has made the distinction in his Cabbalism between mystagogues, madmen, and hard-working seekers of concrete knowledge, he here makes the distinction between Imagination and fantasy. Finally the shreds of theory which appeared and disappeared in Yeats's work in the 'nineties have begun to surface in a coherent pattern. Yeats solidly prefers the Imagination over fantasy, the precise over the vague, just as he consistently prefers Magic over Mysticism; for magic had come to mean control and command over form for him.

ASSERTION OF BELIEF TO CONFRONTATION OF THE ANTI-SELF

Much of this impulse toward concretization may be seen in *Ideas of Good and Evil,* published first in 1903. More accurately than any other source, this set of essays follows Yeats's thought from 1896 to 1903. His own caveats to his friends possibly serve to deflect attention from the volume: To George Russell, on May 14, 1903, he wrote,

> The book is only one half of the orange for I only got a grip on the other half very lately. I am no longer in sympathy with an essay like 'The Autumn of the Body', not that I think the essay untrue. But I think I mistook for a permanent phase of the world what was only a preparation. The close of the last century was full of a strange desire to get out of form, to get to some kind of disembodied beauty, and now it seems to me the contrary impulse has come. I feel about me and in me an impulse to create form, to carry beauty as far as possible.[16]

On the next day, he wrote to John Quinn, expanding on what he had said to Russell and clarifying for us his statement about form:

> The book is too lyrical, too full of aspirations after remote things, too full of desires. Whatever I do from this out will, I think, be more creative. I will express myself, so far as I express myself in criticism at all, by that sort of thought that leads straight to action, straight to some sort of craft. I have always felt that the soul has two movements primarily: one to transcend forms, and the other to create forms. Nietzsche, to whom you have been the first to introduce me, calls these the Dionysiac and the Apollonic, respectively. I think I have to some extent got weary of that wild God Dionysus, and I am hoping that the Far-Darter will come in his place.[17]

The latter statement has been particularly cited in documentation of the time at which Yeats began reading Nietzche; and much of the shift in the direction of his work has been attributed to this reading. But, as Yeats's prose fiction of the 'nineties indicates, he was long concerned over his tendency to seek 'disembodied beauty'. His twin statements to Russell and Quinn do not represent his first impulse toward a more definite form, but they do indicate his consciousness of a need to wipe out of his own work the 'too lyrical' aspects of it. He felt trapped in his own cloud and foam.

In 1897, in 'The Celtic Element in Literature', he had stated that:

I will . . . say that literature dwindles to a mere chronicle of circumstance, or passionless fantasies, and passionless meditations, unless it is constantly flooded with the passions and beliefs of ancient times, and that of all the fountains of the passions and beliefs of ancient times in Europe, . . . the Celtic alone has been for centuries close to the main river of European literature.[18]

He added a note in 1924 to the essay which said, 'I should have added as an alternative that the supernatural may at any moment create new myths, but I was timid'. Yeats was timid throughout the 'nineties and especially about the supernatural. The problem with essays like 'The Autumn of the Body' and 'The Celtic Element in Literature' is not that he ceased to believe in his own statements; he simply did not make them directly enough to suit his later confidence. By looking back at his life through his own eyes in *Autobiographies,* by examining his unpublished diaries and manuscripts, we can see how deeply involved he was in Magic, mysticism, mythology and the supernatural. But in his poetry and in his essays, especially before 1900, he thrusts seldom and parries much with these issues.

After the 'most difficult year' of 1900, Yeats began to assert his own beliefs with greater security. In 'The Symbolism of Poetry', written in that year, he states indirectly, but far more clearly than before, his correlation between the forms of poetry and his magical experiments:

All sounds, all colours, all forms, either because of their preordained energies or because of long associations, evoke indefinable and yet precise emotions, or as I prefer to think, call down among us certain disembodied powers, whose footsteps over our hearts we call emotions; and when sound, and colour, and form are in a musical relation, a beautiful relation to one another, they become, as it were, one sound, one colour, one form and evoke an emotion that is made out of their distinct evocations and yet is one emotion. The same relation exists between all portions of every work of art, whether it be an epic or a song, and the more perfect it is and the more various and numerous the elements that have flowed into its perfection, the more powerful will be the emotion, the power, the god it calls among us.[19]

Yeats is suggesting, in what has been a famous and unexamined theoretical statement, that art, 'whether it be an epic or a song', functions as do the Cabbalistic symbols given him by Mathers. As a *Mandala,* or magical symbol will evoke emotions, powers, gods, so will any work of art call up from within such powerful responses. The more perfect the form of the work of art, the more powerful will be the responses it evokes. He still refers vaguely to 'disembodied powers', but he will not for long.

Shortly afterwards in 'What is "Popular Poetry"?' (1901), he wrote:

> I learned from the people themselves before I learned it from any book, that they cannot separate the idea of an art or a craft from the idea of a cult with ancient technicalities and mysteries. *They can hardly separate mere learning from Witchcraft*, and are fond of words and verses that keep half their secret to themselves. Indeed, it is certain that before the counting-house had created a new class and a new art without breeding and without ancestry and set this art and this class between the hut and the castle, and between the hut and the cloister, the art of the people was as closely mingled with the art of the coteries as was the speech of the people that delighted in rhythmical animation, in idiom, in images, in words full of far-off suggestion, with the unchanging speech of poets.[20]

Yeats is fascinated with 'words and verses that keep half their secret to themselves', partially because of his own earlier methods, partially because of his timidity about expressing his belief in the connection between the supernatural and art. If he describes the suggestive power of language as he has heard it from the country people without concrete examples of his own to offer, best to imply it is all a mystery. But Yeats gives himself away: what he has been learning from the people about poetry is that its traditions in Ireland are linked to the 'idea of a cult with ancient technicalities', and further, with previously uncharacteristic daring, he links art and learning in Ireland to 'Witchcraft'. Implicit in this statement is the belief that only the elite of 'the castle' and the select of 'the hut' will (or did) understand art so based on cults, technicalities, mysteries and witchcraft. The hated Catholic middle class 'without breeding and without ancestry' has wedged materialism between the naturally affinitive art of the people and of the coteries. Yeats will seek with his art to bring 'Everything down to that sole test again,/Dream of the noble and the beggar-man'.[21] He did not, as so many critics have believed, develop his elitist ideas as a result of senility; they were present almost from the beginning of his realization that Catholic bourgeois Ireland rejected him and all that he represented. But his faith in the noble and the beggar-man did not stem merely from rejection.

His observation, that only the elite and the peasants in Ireland valued the traditions of the Celtic past, was accurate. In 'Ireland and the Arts', he dreamed of having 'Ireland recreate the ancient arts, the arts as they were understood in Judea, in India, in Scandinavia, in Greece and Rome, in every ancient land; . . . ' and this done, 'The Irish race would have become a chosen race, one of the pillars that uphold the world'.[22] But it would be Yeats (and Synge and Lady Gregory by his count) who would work at this recreation of the ancient arts, not violently politicized Ireland. He would turn even his relative isolation in his culture to advantage. Writing to Fiona Macleod in 1901, he says:

> To some extent I have an advantage over you in having a very fierce nation to write for. I have to make everything very hard and clear, as it were. It is like riding a wild horse. If one's hands fumble or one's knees loosen one is thrown.[23]

To ride the wild horse, to begin 'to make everything very hard and clear', would require courage, the courage to state with clarity and conviction the beliefs upon which his future work would be based, and in 1901, Yeats wrote what would be the most difficult of his essays for critics to accept, at least until he wrote his argument from eugenics in *On the Boiler*. In 'Magic', he stated that:

> I believe in the practice and philosophy of what we have agreed to call magic, in what I must call the evocation of spirits, though I do not know what they are, in the power of creating magical illusion, in the visions of truth in the depths of the mind when the eyes are closed; and I believe in three doctrines, which have, as I think, been handed down from early times and been the foundation of nearly all magical practices. These doctrines are: –
> (1) That the borders of our minds are ever shifting, and that many minds can flow into one another, as it were, and create or reveal a single mind, a single energy.
> (2) That the borders of our memories are as shifting, and that our memories are a part of one great memory, the memory of Nature herself.
> (3) That this great mind and great memory can be evoked by symbols.[24]

As we have seen from Yeats's experience in the 'nineties, none of these beliefs, in the practice and philosophy of magic, in the evocation of spirits, in the power of creating magical illusion, in visions, is new. The public statement, however, was a radical break with his past. His three doctrines which he had tested in solitude and with others using *mandalas* and telepathy, are basic to understanding his work.

Yeats would state and restate his belief, would examine and add to what he wrote in 1901. He will in *Per Amica Silentia Lunae* and *A Vision* complicate his 1901 statement almost past our understanding. But he will never revoke this basic credo.

It would be difficult to cite any one of the three doctrines as most important; clearly they depend upon each other in almost syllogistic progression. But the third, 'That this great mind and great memory can be evoked by symbols', connects most directly to Yeats's poetic practice, as his further commentary in 'Magic' makes evident. He writes:

> Have not poetry and music arisen, as it seems, out of the sounds the enchanters made to help their imaginations to enchant, to charm, to bind with a spell themselves and the passers-by? These very words, a chief part of all praises of music or poetry, still cry to us their origin. The musician or poet enchants and charms and binds with a spell his own mind when he would enchant the mind of others. . . .[25]

So, for Yeats, words themselves have become the evocative symbols in the ancient, ritualistic art of poetry. To open himself to the great mind, the great memory, for which he has found support in 'magical tradition of many countries', in 'Indian books', in 'folk-lore', and in 'the Prophetic Books of William Blake', he will use word symbols, numerological symbols, the geometric symbols of Cabbalistic tradition, for, as he says:

> I cannot now think symbols less than the greatest of all powers whether they are used consciously by the masters of magic, or half unconsciously by their successors, the poet, the musician and the artist.

He goes on to define what he means by symbols, stating that he can no longer 'distinguish between' inherent symbols and arbitrary symbols. 'Whether their power has arisen out of themselves, or whether it has an arbitrary origin, matters little', he tells us, 'for they act, as I believe, because the Great Memory associates them with certain events and moods and persons'. He continues,

> Whatever the passions of man have gathered about, becomes a symbol in the Great Memory, and in the hands of him who has the secret it is a worker of wonders, a caller-up of angels or

of devils. The symbols are of all kinds, for everything in heaven or earth has its association, momentous or trivial, in the Great Memory, and one never knows what forgotten event may have plunged it, like the toadstool and the ragweed, into the great passions.

As Stevens says 'a wave is a force and not the water of which it is composed, which is never the same',[26] so Yeats says a symbol is a force, a power, which gains its strength from the Great Memory, and may be manifested in the momentous, the trivial, in associations which connect to 'main symbols (symbolic roots, as it were) [which] draw upon associations which are beyond the reach of the individual "subconsciousness" '.[27]

Yeats's root symbols differ from Platonic ideals in that they are within us and accessible to 'him who has the secret', to the master of magic, and even in a half-conscious fashion to the poet, the musician, the artist. He was not content to limit himself to the half-conscious use of symbols in his exploration of the great mind, the great memory. In addition to his semi-inheritance as a poet, he sought for the most part of his life to become a 'master of magic' himself, at least partly because once he had witnessed the tragic generation's destruction because of half-consciousness, his goal could be nothing less than total consciousness. He wrote 'Magic' not to declare himself a magician but to explain for the first time how much the magician and the poet were one. 'I must write or be of no account to any cause, good or evil', he concludes. 'I must commit what merchandise of wisdom I have to this ship of written speech, and . . . I have many a time watched it put out to sea with not less alarm when all the speech was rhyme.'[28]

Though the impulse toward publicly stating his belief in magic may have been partially connected to Yeats's determination to fight the prevailing decadence in his style,[29] to drive from himself the demon of sentimental vagueness, the support he found in Douglas Hyde's 1899 *A Literary History of Ireland* may have provided the final piece of courage he needed at the moment. Hyde's definition of the roots of poetry, of the poet and his ancient connection to magical ritual is strongly Druidic in tone. Hyde had written that the Druids were not an established order in Ireland as they had been in Britain and on the continent, that they had no set rites of worship or regular priesthood.[30] 'Druidh' in ancient Gaelic was equivalent to 'poet and magician'; and later Druid meant 'poet, magician and teacher'. The druid/poet practised incantation in order to make revealed to himself what he

ASSERTION OF BELIEF TO CONFRONTATION OF THE ANTI-SELF

wished to discover from the great soul, and served as an intermediary between man and the invisible powers. They could prophesy, worshipped the sun and the moon, and believed in metempsychosis. Columcille, the Irish saint who had so fascinated Yeats in the 'nineties, was taught by a Druid whom he called 'son of God'. Yeats knew from his magical studies that the Druids and their practices were considered Oriental and Egyptian in origin; surely he knew also of their connection to magic and poetry. But Hyde's *History* set forth the tradition as a valid and respectable part of Ireland's past. Yeats, who had been seeking a way to avoid the excesses of mysticism, and an identity as an Irish poet, must have welcomed Hyde's statement. He, the Anglo-Irishman with his 'occult' practices and magical beliefs, was not only a poet but a poet in the ancient Celtic tradition.

The Christ-like status of the druids also appealed to him, for in 1901, the year in which he wrote 'Magic', Yeats also wrote a short pamphlet, *Is the Order of the R.R. and A.C. to Remain a Magical Order?*[31] R.R. and A.C. stood for *Roseae Rubeae Et Aureae Crucis*, the Latin name of the Rosicrucian Cabbalistic group beset by the possibility of a split following the trouble with Mathers and Crowley. Yeats argued for the preservation of the order on the grounds that a 'great Adept', or master of magic, might come from the order, and,

> If any were to become great among us, he would do so, not by shutting himself up from us in any 'group', but by bringing himself near to continual sacrifice . . . continual miracle. . . . If we preserve the unity of the Order . . . the Order will become a single very powerful talisman, creating in us and in the world about us such moods and circumstances as may best serve the magical life. . . .[32]

He is the one among them who will become the great Adept; he will do so in an Order he believes nearly divine in power and extension, a kind of mystical body of Christ. In assuming responsibility for keeping together this 'single very powerful talisman', Yeats came close to believing in himself as a druidic 'son of God'. As his unpublished manuscripts indicate, the idea was to preoccupy him privately for years.

Yeats signed several of his later works, including the entire first draft of *A Vision*, with the letters I.A.O., which are the three letters derived in a Cabbalistic ceremony from INRI. I.A.O. means the one who has reached enlightenment and stands in the position of a 'son of God'. His attempts to keep the order together so that the 'great Adept' might rise from it were successful and the group adopted a new name – *Stella Matutina*.

Despite his attempts at strength and certainty in his dealings with the Cabbalists and in his essays, Yeats's poetry from 1899 to 1902 reflects little of the new man. *In the Seven Woods* (1903) contains only one poem, 'Adam's Curse',[33] to suggest the writer who finally got 'toadstools and ragweed' into his prose. As he has admitted his belief in Magic, Yeats asserts in this poem for the first time a theme which will reappear in his later work – the difficulty of writing poetry. In the first stanza, he writes:

> We sat together at one summer's end,
> That beautiful mild woman, your close friend,
> And you and I, and talked of poetry.
> I said: 'A line will take us hours maybe;
> Yet if it does not seem a moment's thought,
> Our stitching and unstitching has been naught.
> Better go down upon your marrow-bones
> And scrub a kitchen pavement, or break stones
> Like an old pauper, in all kinds of weather;
> For to articulate sweet sounds together
> Is to work harder than all these, and yet
> Be thought an idler by the noisy set
> Of bankers, schoolmasters, and clergymen
> The martyrs call the world'. (I. 1–14)

The poem shifts into a discussion of the labour beauty requires, the artificial strivings of love, and finally we are left with a self-pitying group 'as weary-hearted as that hollow moon' (V. 38). Adam's curse is ambiguous; it may be that since the fall nothing beautiful is possible without labour, labour which will be unappreciated; or it may be that since Adam, all the labour is for naught because Time wipes out the illusions created by poet, beautiful woman or lover.

But within 'Adam's Curse', Yeats has written some of his first direct, concrete statements too: 'Better go down upon your marrow-bones/ And scrub a kitchen pavement, or break stones/ Like an old pauper', and 'Our stitching and unstitching has been naught/ . . . if it does not seem a moment's thought'.[34] He issues his first poetic condemnation of the bourgeoisie, though it is muted by comparison with his fury in *Responsibilities,* which was to come later. In an attempt to break the soft constrictions of accepted structures in his early poetry, he experiments to produce a clear dry sound. Perhaps 'Adam's Curse' represents an attempt at reproducing common speech as Ellmann suggests,[35] but the poem exhibits more than an experiment in diction. Though 'Adam's Curse' appears to be less 'stitched' than Yeats's early poetry, it is perhaps more laboured than any of the previous work. The conservative use of heroic couplets, apparent to the eye, muted when read, makes the poem precisely what Yeats suggests it should be: so stitched *and* unstitched that it seems 'a moment's thought'. For its confidently honest diction and its successfully employed form, 'Adam's Curse' must be marked as evidence of Yeats's growth toward his mature style.[36]

But among his other poetry from 1902 to almost 1910, 'Adam's Curse' is exceptional. If we see him only as a poet, these years were most bleak, and with that isolation made, most major critics have pointed to Maud Gonne as the source of the problem. As the argument goes, Maud's marriage to Major MacBride in 1903 threw Yeats into a debilitating depression which kept him from his poetry for years. This argument weakens when we look at what Yeats accomplished during these years: in 1903 he published *Ideas of Good and Evil* and *In the Seven Woods;* in 1904 he started the Abbey Theatre and toured America; in 1906 he published *Poems 1889-1905,* including *The Shadowy Waters, The King's Threshold,* and *On Baile's Strand;* in 1908, at forty-two, he saw the publication of his *Collected Works;* during these years, in addition to the plays included in the 1906 *Poems,* he wrote and re-wrote *The Pot of Broth* (1904), *The Hour Glass* (prose, 1903), and *Deirdre* (1907); he also revised, with Lady Gregory, *The Celtic Twilight*[37] and *Stories of Red Hanrahan;* and he wrote several articles, many of them until recently uncollected.

Yeats was undoubtedly disturbed by Maud's marriage but critics have too long pointed to her alleged perfidy, ultimately at Yeats's expense. Ellmann, for instance, refers to the affair as the "obsession" of a thirty-seven year old man who had "remained in his love affair a wide-eyed boy',[38] with scarcely concealed condescension. As Ellmann has pointed out, the lost years of Yeats's poetic life may only be speculatively judged; and if we avoid obscuring our view with visions of Maud, we can make other suggestions about his path in those years.

First, the idea of an Irish theatre had been important to Yeats from the late 'nineties. Given the possibility of influencing Irish culture through the Abbey Theatre, he could hardly have refused the experiment[39] made possible by Annie Horniman's support.[40] In *Samhain: 1904,*[41] he writes with strength and conviction uncharacteristic of the love-sick boy-man, explaining his goals for the Irish Theatre:

YEATS AND MAGIC: THE EARLIER WORKS

> I would not be trying to form an Irish National Theatre if I did not believe that there existed in Ireland, whether in the minds of a few people or of a great number I do not know, an energy of thought about life itself, a vivid sensitiveness as to the reality of things, powerful enough to overcome all those phantoms of the night. Everything calls up its contrary, unreality calls up reality, and, besides, life here has been sufficiently perilous to make men think. I do not think it a national prejudice that makes me believe we are harder, a more masterful race than the comfortable English of our time, and that this comes from an essential nearness to reality of those few scattered people who have the right to call themselves the Irish race. It is only in the exceptions, in the few minds where the flame has burnt, . . . that one can see the permanent character of a race.

Yeats has totally identified with those few scattered people who have the right to call themselves the Irish race: he is one of the exceptional, few minds, vividly sensitive to the reality of things, and his propagandistic tone in this piece reflects part of his intention in devoting himself to the Irish Theatre. To lead, to shape, to tap the energy of 'sufficiently perilous' Ireland, Yeats will take a calculated risk and devote himself almost totally to drama for a time, but, as could be said about every move he made in the twentieth century, his purpose was not single.

He was painfully, persistently, aware of the split between his desires for a clear, hard, direct style and his still too soft and vague performance. He had to act radically if he was to infuse into his poetry the honesty and courage he was learning to express in his prose. To do this he consciously began serving an apprenticeship in drama. As he explains:

> What attracts me to drama is that it is, in the most obvious way, what all the arts are upon a last analysis. A farce and a tragedy are alike in this, that they are a moment of intense life. An action is taken out of all other actions; it is reduced to its simplest form, or at any rate to as simple a form as it can be brought to without our losing the sense of its place in the world. The characters that are involved in it are freed from everything that is not part of that action; . . . it is in the more important kinds, an activity of the souls of the characters, it is an energy, an eddy of life purified from everything but itself. The dramatist must picture life in action, with an unpreoccupied mind, as the musician pictures it in sound and the sculptor in form.[42]

He has moved far from the days when he and his Rhymer friends advocated a gem-like purity of emotion; now Yeats seeks to learn how to portray moments of intense life, the energy of the soul, life in action. To do this as a dramatist, he will have to work with an 'unpreoccupied mind', stripping action to its 'simplest form'. If he can succeed in this attempt, his statement implies, perhaps he can learn to strip and energize his poetry, for in the same essay, 'First Principles', he concludes,

> There are two kinds of poetry, and they are comingled in all the greatest works. When the tide of life sinks low . . . the pictures make us sorrowful. We share the poet's separation from what he describes. It is life in the mirror, and our desire for it is the desire of the lost souls for God; but when Lucifer stands up among his friends, when Villon sings his dead ladies so gallant a rhythm, when Timon makes his epitaph, we feel no sorrow, for life herself has made one of her eternal gestures, has called up into our hearts her energy that is eternal delight.[43]

Yeats's early poetry had been 'life in the mirror' reflecting his separation from what he described; but, now, Yeats, whose name in the Order was *Demon est Deus Inversus,* would invert the sorrow and separation to celebrate heroically, as did Lucifer, Villon and Timon, the 'eternal gestures of life', which call up 'in our hearts her energy which is eternal delight'. First, he will attempt this in drama, and finally he will begin to write in a style for which he has searched for over twenty years.

Productive as were the years from 1904 to 1909, they were also difficult. Beginning the Abbey Theatre was a struggle which exacerbated Yeats's scars from the 'nineties. The Nationalist Clubs refused to support the effort and Yeats aimed at first for 'the general public'.[44] At his strongest, he wrote to Russell that 'It is a long fight but that is the sport of it'.[45] At times he felt himself freed, powerful, moving 'downwards upon life',[46] as a result of his work with the theatre and his deepening study of astrology and Eastern meditation.[47] But as the wild, dark portrait of him by Augustus John indicates, Yeats was overburdened and troubled during this time. The *Playboy* riots of 1907 shocked and angered him deeply; he would never forget the proof that the Irish middle class would reject Synge's 'harsh, independent, heroical, clean, wind-swept view of things', in favour of their 'clerical conservatory where the air is warm and damp'.[48] In his mind, the Abbey changed from an effort to attract the public to an enterprise for the benefit of the enthusiastic minority, because, as he bitterly wrote to John Quinn in 1908, 'Pitt decapitated Ireland'.[49]

Yeats's encouragement and support of Synge, as well as his

reaction to the *Playboy* riots, are, above all, indicative of what he wanted from himself. Synge's prose and drama had, almost from its inception, the force and purity Yeats so desired to master for his poetry. When Synge was martyred by the mob, Yeats almost envied him his position, for his own plays were succeeding with the same people who hated *Playboy*. As he unenthusiastically put it in 1908 after *Deirdre,* 'There has not been one hostile voice here and I am now accepted as a dramatist in Dublin'.[50] He loved fame and success and the power they brought with them, but he could not rest until his work was as harsh, independent, heroical and wind-swept as was that of his fellow Anglo-Irishman, Synge.

In 1908, Arthur Symons, Yeats's strongest personal link to the Symboliste tradition, went mad. Having visited him in this state, Yeats wrote in horror that Symons wanted to go to Galway to see Teig the fool, one of his own literary characters; 'God!' was Yeats's succinct judgment of Symons's retreat from reality. The overworked Yeats suffered another breakdown himself and retreated to Coole to work on *The Player Queen* and *The Golden Helmet.* He began a diary, part of which has been published as *Estrangement,* which shows him still angry at those who persecuted Synge. Quoting Goethe, he writes, 'The Irish always seem to me like a pack of hounds dragging down some noble stag'.[51] Most of all, he worried that by 'running at full speed', as he had been, he might have destroyed his talent. 'I often wonder', he records,

> if my talent will ever recover from the heterogeneous labour of these last few years.... I cry out vainly for liberty and have ever less and less inner life.... I thought myself loving neither vice nor virtue; but virtue has come upon me and given me a nation instead of a home. Has it left me any lyrical faculty?[52]

What was to make him gain confidence once again in his talent was the attempt to integrate a new area of meditation and mythology into his work. Since about 1900, some of the Golden Dawn members had been investigating Buddhism, and during the same years he was devoting himself to the Abbey, Yeats was exploring the topic. His unpublished papers indicate correspondence with Alan Bennett, a former Theosophist and Golden Dawn member,[53] who emigrated to Ceylon and Burma to become a Buddhist monk. Yeats does not seem to have been interested in the ascetic aspects of Buddhism; he placed the letter from Bennett in a pocket of the diaries in which he was making notes on Irish gods, the planets, and the zodiac,[54] indicating his connection between Buddhism and the patterns he was attempting to make from Irish myth and legend.

In *Estrangement,* which appears in the Macmillan edition as a series of fifty-five short notes, the connection between what he had learned of Buddhism and his work becomes clear. The first note begins:

> To keep these notes natural and useful to me I must keep one note from leading on to another, that I may not surrender myself to literature. Every note must come as a casual thought, then it will be my life. Neither Christ nor Buddha nor Socrates wrote a book, for to do that is to exchange life for a logical process.[55]

Yeats said of *Discoveries,* a set of short observations and thoughts which parallel those in *Estrangement,* that they were a channel for his philosophy, a channel he felt necessary to keep abstraction out of his work. In the first note of *Estrangement,* he seems to ask us to see the notes in this set in the same way, to view them as separate from 'literature'. We might even posit an anti-intellectualism in the 'Neither Christ nor Buddha nor Socrates wrote a book, for to do that is to exchange life for a logical process', and perhaps go on to surmise that the form of *Estrangement* is a reflection of the disconnected alienation the title seems to indicate. The title may also reflect an extension of his anti-nineteenth century evaluation of the empiricism of his youth, an attitude he had transcended as he recognized the value of magic to him. *Estrangement* surely describes the distance Yeats felt himself to have strayed from his desire not 'to elevate' or 'educate' Ireland but 'to make them understand my vision'.[56] Once again, though, Yeats's experiments in prose reflect not only the complexity of his intentions but also a shift in consciousness which will not become immediately apparent in his poetry or in his drama.

From 1906, when he was writing *Discoveries,* to 1909, when he wrote *Estrangement,* Yeats had been undergoing initiations into successively higher grades in his Cabbalistic Order,[57] learning and experiencing more and more complex rituals, rituals which do not apparently connect to each other but exist in deliberate and necessary progression. He had been practising Buddhist meditation, short apparently isolated structures which also relate to each other by subtle valence. His notes in *Estrangement* reflect the same kind of formal pattern as his Cabbalistic rituals and Buddhist meditations. The sections are anything but 'natural' and though they do not seem to lead on from one to the other, they form a complex web without a nucleus, held together by the force they exert upon each other. Yeats was not attempting to avoid literature as he seems to imply, he does not want to *surrender* to the unconscious forces of literary tradition. *Estrangement*, like his rituals and Buddhist meditations, is a struggle toward consciousness, not a flight from it into a mask which obscures reality. And the second note concludes so, saying that 'Style, personality – deliberately adopted and therefore a mask –'[58] is the only way to escape the machine that is logic, or, more accurately, the only way to discover the reality of the self.

In Yeats's thinking, a mask is a second self which exists in creative conflict with the first self – his notes are set up so that they exert creative tension upon each other, mimicking the concept of mask. As he moved farther into the occult, he began to know what he would take from the East, and how it would relate to what he took from Ireland. He speculated on the root connection between the mythologies of East and West, asking 'Was the Bhagavad Gita the "scenario" from which the Gospels were made'?[59] But then he moved to his clearest statement to date of the difference between East and West:

> By implication the philosophy of Irish faery lore declares that all power is from the body, all intelligence from the spirit. Western civilization, religion and magic insist on power and therefore on body, and hence these three doctrines – efficient rule – the Incarnation – thaumaturgy. Eastern thought answers to these with indifference to rule, scorn of the flesh, contemplation of the formless. Western minds who follow the Eastern way become weak and vapoury, because unfit for the work forced upon them by Western life. Every Symbol is an invocation which produces its equivalent expression in all worlds. The Incarnation invoked modern science and modern efficiency, and individualized emotion. It produced a solidification of all those things that grow from individual will. The historical truth of the Incarnation is indifferent, though the belief in that truth was essential to the power of the invocation. All civilization is held together by the suggestions of an invisible hypnotist – by artificially created illusions. The knowledge of reality is always in some measure a secret knowledge.[60]

This statement rivals in complexity any of Yeats's other prose formulations. It is difficult, not in the the sense that sections of *A Vision* are, but in the labyrinth of implications it contains. It is central to any assessment of his development as thinker and poet, revealing him to be in 1909 much closer to his mature beliefs than has been previously supposed. First, he believes the key difference between East and West is in the place assigned to the will within their respective cosmologies and theologies. Mythology is the vehicle Yeats has used to ascertain the importance of magic, power and the body in Western civilization. Recognizing the roots of modern science and efficiency, he is no longer tempted to despair or escapism. His magic is unlike the mysticism of the East, as it was practised by his friend Russell, with resultant vapourization of his mind, which lay passively before reality. Nor was it like the magic of Mathers and Crowley which was used to change, to transform external reality. Yeats's magic will be a method used to invoke the reality which is within the individual body or consciousness and within the Great Mind. Thus, the Incarnation, the historical truth of which is unimportant to Yeats, is essential to his conception of history, personality, power and more specifically, magical power.

Living in Catholic Ireland, he surely knew the phrase used in description of the Incarnation: it was the moment 'when the word was made flesh'. According to the belief which Yeats sees as a central imprinting factor in the formation of Western consciousness, God spoke and through the symbol of the dove, he invoked the Incarnation of Christ within the body of Mary. The Incarnation, as a specific kind of thaumaturgy, or miracle, or magic, depends not upon transforming reality, but upon invoking from within a human body, a divinity. Yeats, with his own Christ-like inclinations, is practising in *Estrangement* the power of the invisible hypnotist, the magician or thaumaturgist who by the 'gathering up of an entire web of influences',[61] by using the symbols/words, by building an invisible pattern with his seemingly disconnected notes, shows himself possessed of that knowledge of reality which is 'always in some measure a secret knowledge'. And, his attempt will be to invoke the same kind of divinity from within us at moments as God invoked in Mary in the moment of Incarnation. Efficient rule is a metaphor for the ritual, practised by the thaumaturgist or magician, practised to invoke, as did the Incarnation, that which exists within the individual mind which is connected, he believes, to the Great Mind. Yeats suggests not only that he may be a new incarnation, but that his poems, if they succeed, will work as microcosmic incarnations.

Estrangement is not simply the record of a man alienated from his time and his poetry; it represents a rethinking of his philosophy at a higher level of consciousness than Yeats had previously achieved. He believed he had to go through the years of the Abbey and continue his Cabbalistic practices if he was to break with the role of 'traditional poet' he had played in the 'nineties. But by the time he wrote *Estrangement* he was on his way not backward to the old poetry, but downward upon life, from which he would write poetry, based not upon a 'Kind of Holy City of the imagination',[62] but upon the soul of the individual human being, the soul connected to the power that is his body, and thus, to divinity. By 1909, he was completely cynical about the sterility of Protestant Ireland and the sentimental clericalism of Catholic Ireland. But he was approaching his greatest confidence about his own powers and their connection to the supernatural.

In the awesome patterning he was learning to exploit, he ends *Estrangement* with a ghost story:

> I told my sister that I was to spend the night in the K—— street haunted house. She said, 'O, I know about that house. I saw a furniture van there one day and furniture going in, and ten days after, the house was empty again; and somebody I know was passing by in the early morning and saw an old woman on the windowsill, clinging to the sash. She was the caretaker. The ghost had driven her out and there was a policeman trying to get her down. But the pious Protestants say that there is no ghost or anything but the young novices in the Convent opposite "screaming in the night time".'[63]

Yeats seeks to confront the haunted house with its ghost. Unlike those who run from it in fear, or piously denounce it as the product of mysterious and virulent Catholicism, he believes in the ghost. He is not estranged from the reality of the haunted individual consciousness; he will neither run from it nor deny it, but confront it and write of it with the power of the magician. 'Great Art', he was to write in 1910, 'chills at first by its coldness or its strangeness, by what seems capricious,' like the ghost story, 'and yet it is from these qualities it has authority, as though it had fed on locusts and wild honey. The imaginative writer shows us the world . . . as we were Adam and this the first morning.'[64]

'The Death of Synge', the other published portion of his 1909 diary, indicates how far Yeats had come in the struggle with 'the infinite pain of self-realization',[65] which was the basis of his consciousness as an artist. His assessment of Synge was thorough, perhaps more so than that of any other of his contemporaries, and his reaction to Synge's death, at least in his published writings, seems exceedingly cold and admirably conscious. Synge, in

ASSERTION OF BELIEF TO CONFRONTATION OF THE ANTI-SELF

whom 'the external self, the mask, the *persona,* was a shadow; character . . . all',[66] who loved the wildness and coldness he found in the Western Irish, taught Yeats more about style than any other writer, including Pound, whom Yeats did not meet until three years after Synge's death. Synge, he said on April 4, 1909,

> was a solitary, undemonstrative man, never asking pity, nor complaining, nor seeking sympathy . . . all folded up in brooding intellect, knowing nothing of new books and newspapers, reading the great masters alone; and he was but the more hated because he gave his country what it needed, an unmoved mind where there is a perpetual Last Day, a trumpeting, and coming up to judgement.[67]

He was 'proud and lonely, almost as proud of his old blood as of his genius',[68] and had in his style 'imaginative richness and yet . . . the sting and tang of reality'.[69] Yeats was later to say that he loved 'proud and lonely things',[70] especially the proud and lonely Synge who was the master ironist he so needed as a model. He never seems to have doubted that his was the greater mind, that his vision and talent were more important than Synge's. While Synge said, 'We should unite stoicism, ascetism and ecstasy. Two of them have often come together, but the three never',[71] it was Yeats who would bring this strange triad together, he who would achieve in his poetry the cold passion he described in 1909, saying that passionate intensity touches 'the unchanging rock, the secret place beyond life.' 'Passion', he continues, 'looks beyond mankind and asks no pity, not even of God. It realizes, substantiates, attains, scorns, governs, and is most mighty when it passes from our sight'.[72] Cold passion cannot be paraphrased nor defined, as Yeats seems to have known. It is a metaphor for the most arrogant and powerful simplicity any poet has ever sought. By 1909, he had integrated himself, had learned enough, so that he could assert with absolute confidence that 'A good writer should be so simple that he has no faults, only sins'.[73]

Yeats understood consciously what Synge partially intuited, that

> . . . the nobleness of the arts is in the mingling of contraries, the extremity of sorrow, the extremity of joy, perfection of personality, the perfection of its surrender, overflowing turbulent energy, and marmorean stillness; and its red rose opens at the trysting-place of mortal and immortal, time and eternity. No new man has ever plucked that rose, or found that trysting place, for he could but come to the understanding of himself, to the

mastery of unlocking words, after long frequenting of the great Masters, hardly without ancestral memory of the like.[74]

These lines ring of the Rosicrucian Magician, as Yeats desires not to reconcile opposites, as Ellmann says,[75] but to mingle them, to arrange words as a master does, unlocking them. The rose he worshipped in the 'nineties, he now seeks to pluck at the point where mortal and immortal, time and eternity, cross. If he was to seize the rose, he had to be 'very conscious' and 'very deliberate', learning first to come to a complete understanding of himself.

Part II

Part of Yeats's attempt to break through to a new level of consciousness and self understanding is reflected in his revived interest in Spiritualism in 1909. He had not attended a seance since the late 'eighties when he had been apparently frightened by his experience. Especially beginning in 1911, he approached the area of Spiritualism with renewed interest and courage, as the final passage of the Macmillan[76] *Estrangement* suggests he would. To know himself, Yeats felt he had to come to terms with his other self, or mask, and in 1911, at the house of an American medium, he confronted a voice which claimed to be his mask, his other self, with him since childhood. The voice called itself Leo Africanus, on whom Yeats checked and who he found to be a sixteenth-century Moorish writer and explorer who had been a captive at the court of Pope Leo X. As he was to do later with the masks of Robartes and Aherne, Yeats carried on a correspondence between himself and Africanus in deliberately disguised handwriting. The unpublished manuscript indicates that much of *A Vision* is connected to the Leo Africanus experience and that Yeats saw Leo as the conjunction of East and West within himself that he had sought for years. Spiritualism and especially Leo Africanus were powerful stimuli in Yeats's poetic career, for upon discovery of the other self connecting East and West, conscious and unconscious mind, he wrote the first draft of one of his major poems, 'Ego Dominus Tuus'. The poem has been previously dated by Ellmann as 1915[77] and was not published until 1917 with *Per Amica Silentia Lunae,* the obvious genesis of *A Vision*.[78] An unpublished manuscript[79] dates this important poem to 1912, and stands as a measure of the distance Yeats had travelled by that date toward his mature thought. The draft of the poem, as is the case with most of the longer drafts of his work available to us, reveals much about the intentions behind the poem not immediately apparent in the final version. The 1912 draft begins:

EGO DOMINUS TUUS

Hic   On the grey sand beside the shallow sea
         Under your old wind-beaten tower, where still
         ~~The~~, your lamp burns on beside the open book
         ~~That Michael Robartes left, as in your boyhood~~
         (several lines unreadable, crossed out)

Ille   By the help of images
         I could call up my anti-self, summon all
         ~~That I have least looked on, (————)~~
         That I have least handled, look upon them all
         Because I am most weary of myself.

Hic   (two lines unreadable, crossed out)
         I'd rather seek a form of myself

Ille   ~~This is our modern aim (————)~~
         This is our modern Hope and by its light
         on gentle minds or on sincere heart (————)
         our sensitive minds (————)
         the
         our sensitive minds   the lost   the sheer fun
         The (————)
         The gay nonchalance of shaping palm.
         (————)
         when we chose,
         When we write, in forms' chisel in a pen
         (————)
         ~~When we have chosen,~~ pen, pallet or brush
         We are but critics: or but half create
         (————)
         (————)
         ~~know~~
         ~~mine~~ (————)
         We are but timid entangled (   ) abashed
         Knowing one line we hold this far away
         ~~being, timid entangled and abashed~~
         ~~because this line has held us far away~~

All of the speech attributed here to Ille is crossed out with a diagonal line and Yeats begins again:

        this is our modern hope and by this light
        we have found the gentle sensitive mind

~~and lost our nonchalant hand~~
and lost the old nonchalance of this hand
whether we choose chisel, or pen or brush
we are but critics; or but half create
~~because~~
~~Being,~~ timid, entangled and abashed and ⟨empty⟩
~~Because of a line has held it far away~~
lacking the countenance of our friends

Ille's speech here is very close to the final text, as is most of what is readable in the first draft of the beginning ten lines of text. Yeats's revisions are significant in terms of the concretization and directness he was seeking: Ille's first speech, for example, in the draft, without excisions noted, reads:

> By the help of images
> I could call up my anti-self, summon all
> That I have least handled, look upon them all
> Because I am most weary of myself.

Yeats dropped the last weak line, excises 'could' and changes the images to 'image'. Finally the lines read:

> By the help of an image
> I call to my own opposite, summon all
> That I have handled least, least looked upon.

The timid entanglement of the first draft statement has been stripped of tentativeness and self-pity, and 'anti-self' has been simplified for the introductory exchange to 'my own opposite'. In the draft, though, Yeats is clearly describing the occult experiment which led to the summoning of Leo Africanus; in the final text, he makes the seeking of one's opposite seem a less ritualistic activity.

But even as he writes those first lines, Yeats is troubled by his own timidity in the face of the modern world. It was an old and familiar problem to him and in the draft he worries about losing 'the old nonchalance', about being 'empty', the word he circles in the draft. Ille worries about a line that 'held it far away'; 'it' perhaps being courage, directness, or creative power. The 'line' is most likely the clever 'we are but critics, or but half create', which seems to have come out whole on the first try as did many of Yeats's most memorable lines. The argument developing in the draft is one Yeats wishes to avoid; he does not want to appeal to the 'modern' mind, which he too possesses, or to evade the problems of magic and art by indulging in sentimental, self-

ASSERTION OF BELIEF TO CONFRONTATION OF THE ANTI-SELF

punishing meditation upon emptiness and sterility. As there is a logical break between lines 17 and 18 in the final draft, there is a clear break in the manuscript at this point. It has long been noted that Hic and Ille do not seem to be contradicting each other but rather complementing each other's statements. Hic's response to Ille's worry about modern times seems in the final version to be a statement we might have expected from Ille who has been seeking his opposite. In the draft of the poem, from this point on, Hic's speeches are labelled 'Ille', and Ille's are labelled 'Hic'. The break we have sensed, the complementary nature of the two characters' dialogue is present in the draft. Yeats continues:

    Ille   and yet
              He that of all the writers of the world
              H̶a̶s̶ ̶m̶o̶s̶t̶ ̶m̶o̶v̶e̶d̶
                                  or comixed
              Has moved man combined magic and a belief?
                  m̶i̶x̶e̶d̶
              Dante, O̶ ̶u̶t̶t̶e̶r̶l̶y̶ so utterly found himself
              (two lines unreadable, crossed out)
              t̶h̶a̶t̶ ̶I̶ ̶c̶a̶n̶ ̶s̶e̶e̶ ̶h̶i̶s̶ ̶f̶a̶c̶e̶ ̶t̶o̶d̶a̶y̶
              t̶h̶i̶s̶ ̶h̶i̶s̶ ̶f̶a̶c̶e̶ ̶I̶ ̶c̶a̶n̶ ̶s̶e̶e̶ ̶i̶n̶ ̶t̶h̶e̶ ̶m̶i̶n̶d̶s̶ ̶e̶y̶e̶.
              That face (   ) I can see his hollow cheek
              more truly than any face in the world
              But that of Christ.
    Hic   Yet did he find himself
              o̶r̶ ̶w̶a̶s̶ ̶t̶h̶e̶ ̶(̶ ̶ ̶ ̶ ̶ ̶ ̶ ̶ ̶ ̶ ̶ ̶ ̶ ̶)̶ ̶h̶u̶n̶g̶e̶r̶
              or was it the hunger that made his cheek so faint
              Hunger for what he had, or for some good
              that seemed the most of all possible good.
                        (   ) of the image you have seen.
              Beyond his reach (―――――) t̶h̶e̶ ̶i̶m̶a̶g̶e̶.̶
              B̶e̶s̶i̶d̶e̶ ̶(̶―――――)̶ ̶c̶a̶l̶v̶a̶r̶y̶
              B̶y̶ ̶C̶
              Beside the calvary, the (   )
              that (―――――) kind.
              (̶―――――)̶
              h̶i̶s̶ ̶g̶e̶n̶e̶r̶o̶u̶s̶
              I̶ ̶s̶h̶o̶w̶ ̶a̶ ̶d̶i̶f̶f̶e̶r̶e̶n̶c̶e̶,̶ ̶I̶ ̶t̶h̶i̶n̶k̶ ̶t̶h̶a̶t̶
              I have a different notion, I think
              a terrible image from his opposite
              He made out of his opposite, his anti-self
              All
              He fashioned all others that from beauty
              a spectral jungle, as it (   ) a stony face
              (three lines unreadable, crossed out)

Staring upon the bedouins hair horse roof
(two and a half lines unreadable, crossed out)
From doored and windowed Cliff, or half upturned
among the course grass and the camel dung.
(five lines unreadable, crossed out)
He saw, alone of living men he saw
(one line unreadable, crossed out)
    the learned Heaven
~~All Holy learning~~ in a needles eye.
The heavens succour is a (   ) foot.
He only from the plucking of the apple.
~~Derided and deriding driven out~~
to chisel that star I eat this bitter bread
(one line unreadable, crossed out)
   he
←——————→ measured the unpersuadable justice
He saw
He only found the gathering of the apple
He only found the unpersuadable justice

There seem to be no other available drafts of 'Ego Dominus Tuus', and surely more existed, but the evidence of the first draft is that the above lines, which became lines 18-37 in the final text, were written as a set, separate from lines 1-17 and from what follows. Probably, all of the sets of Hic-Ille dialogue were composed separately on successive occasions. Ille's above speech, which becomes Hic's in the final, indicates that Dante occupied Yeats's mind, at this point in his life, as an artist 'who most moved man' by 'combining', or 'comixing', magic and a belief. Yeats's quibble with himself over the terms, combining and comixing, is significant in that it evidences his previously stated desire not to reconcile contraries, such as Magic and Christianity, but to place them side by side, to take from both and comix or combine as Yin and Yang combine, gaining power from each other. Dante, he suggests, through Ille, was able to combine magic and a belief (a word he hated and thus questioned in the draft) because he had 'so utterly found himself' in finding his anti-self.

Hic complements the statement while seeming to question it. 'Did he find himself', he asks, as he has asked earlier to find 'a form of myself', which becomes 'myself and not an image' in the final version. But Hic answers his own question revealingly: 'I think a terrible image from his opposite he made . . . ', and 'He fashioned all others . . . from . . . that . . . beauty. He saw, alone of living men . . . the learned Heaven in a needles eye'. Not only are Hic's and Ille's questions and problems Yeats's too, but so are Dante's

ASSERTION OF BELIEF TO CONFRONTATION OF THE ANTI-SELF

answers and achievements his. Yeats had said that the artist shows us the world 'as we were Adam and this the first morning',[80] and the imagery carries over into his draft, as he refers to Dante/Yeats 'plucking the apple' of that same first morning. If Yeats has discovered himself in his anti-self as did Dante in a terrible image connected in the draft with a 'bedouins horse hair roof', a bedouin we cannot but connect to Leo Africanus, then he is ready to fashion all others from that same 'spectral jungle'.

Self-conscious self-knowledge which he attributes to himself in the draft – 'to chisel that star I eat this bitter bread' – and to Dante in the final – 'Being mocked by Guido for his lecherous life,/ Derided and deriding, driven out/ To climb that stair and eat that bitter bread' – is the basis of all that he will do in the future. Clearly, Yeats saw himself and Dante as similar figures, both of them exiles, Dante literally and Yeats figuratively, both of them Magician/ poets. Yeats believed he and Dante shared the power in the Western imagination of Christ, the Word Incarnate, who permeates the first draft and is barely mentioned in the final poem.

In the draft, the dialogue then shifts to Ille:

Ille (two lines unreadable, crossed out)
Ille Yet surely there are some that make their art
      out of the no tragic war – lovers of life – impulsive men.
      (half a line unreadable, crossed out)
      Impulsive men that look for happiness
      And sing when they have found it.
Hic   no not sing
      for those that love the world serve it in action
      grow rich, popular and full of influence
      the struggle of the fly in marmalade
      and should they paint or write still in action:
      the rhetorician would deceive his neighbours
      the sentimentalist himself; while art
      is but a vision of reality.
      What can the artist and magician know
      who have seen awakened from the common dream
      But dissipation and despair.

Both of the above speeches, which become lines 38-51 in the final, were scarcely revised. Only the link between artist and Magician which we find so often in Yeats's prose is dropped in the final text, perhaps because of his timidity, perhaps because he knew that in the modern world, he could better play the 'invisible hypnotist' if he underplayed what was an essential connection in his own mind. In any case, the argument of the above exchange is unambiguous: Ille suggests total self-consciousness is not necessary to art, that the tragic war both he and Hic are fighting is somehow escapable, and perhaps damaging to the old nonchalance. Hic reaches his first definite statement in the draft, denying that the war may be avoided. If it is, the impulsive magician/artist, who shares in the same common dream as the conscious magician/artist, will but awaken 'dissipation and despair.' Yeats is arguing strongly for the responsibility of the artist to make the struggle toward total consciousness so that he may convey to his audience a vision of reality, which for him is connected to the 'common dream', the Great Mind, or *Anima Mundi*. The question is rhetorical; an unconscious, impulsive artist and magician will be an irresponsible deceiver, a sentimentalist, or a mere rhetorician.

Ille then proposes an exception to Hic's assertion:

> Ille   yet some
> (four lines crossed through and diagonally cancelled)
> ~~to praise the heart~~ – had Keats a tragic view

Another diagonal line cancels this start, and Yeats tries again:

> Ille   yet some
> (nine lines unreadable, crossed out)
> but that the world and its (   ) form
> and then upon this poet, model or painter
> to praise the heart – had Keats a tragic view

This will evolve to lines 52-53, 'And yet/No one denies to Keats love of the world: /Remember his deliberate happiness,' but all that is clear in the draft is Ille's attempt to cite Keats, a major romantic poet, as a possible exception to the theory Hic has offered. Without clarifying the lines, Yeats tries for Hic's reply:

> Hic   Because he had it (   )
> (three lines unreadable, then all four cancelled
> with a wavy diagonal line)
> We have (   ) call it so
> He made a happy art who knows his mind
> I see a schoolboy with his nose and face
>   ~~white his hand~~
> ~~Pressed to the sweet shop window~~
> Pressed to the sweet shop window – he made an art
>   ~~(   ) Keats~~
> (one line unreadable, crossed out)

ASSERTION OF BELIEF TO CONFRONTATION OF THE ANTI-SELF

>   Being ill bred, ill born and ignorant
>   shut out from its luxury, a work,
>   of most deliberate luxury

All of the above is then cancelled with four diagonal lines, and Yeats continues:

> Hic   He made a happy art who knows his mind?
>   I see a school boy when I think of him
>   his face and nose pressed to the sweet shop window
>   (three lines unreadable, crossed out)
>   Did he not pass into the grave
>   He has gone senses and heart unsatisfied
>   into the grave – ailing and ignorant
>   the ill bred son of a livery stable-keeper
>   Shut out from all the luxury of the world
>   he made luxurious song.

All of Hic's reply is again cancelled with a diagonal wavy line, and Yeats re-writes:

>   for surely –
>   (   )
>   ~~I think that~~ he went down at his grave
>   senses and heart utterly unsatisfied
>   and made though poor, ailing and ignorant
>   shut out from all the luxury of the world
>   luxurious song.

All of these tries will be compressed into lines 54-62 of the final text, but again the argument has been made clear in the draft. Yeats rejects the power of Keats's supposed negative capability. Keats sought not himself but the sweets in the sweet-shop window, the luxury of the world; his poetry is not that of a Magician like Dante; he did not love but rather desired the world – he was a sentimentalist, who died unsatisfied, and by implication, awakened from the common dream but dissipation and despair with his luxurious song. The totally conscious artist discovers himself in discovering his opposite; Keats was merely happy in his art; he did not fight the necessary tragic war.

In the next set, Ille seems to accept Hic's answer and chides him; then Hic replies.

> Ille   But wherefore leave the lamp
>   Burning along beside an open book
>   to make strange characters upon the sand.

>
> A style is found by sedentary toil,
> the imitation of the masters of the art
> by writing and rewriting
>
> Hic   (half a line unreadable crossed out)
> I would find
> not style – for those who truly are not wise
> own nothing but their blind stupefied hearts
> I call to my own image, my own image
> and get my anti-self – the golden image

The last two lines are cancelled by a diagonal wavy line, and Hic continues:

> I call to this mysterious one who yet
> shall walk the wet sand of the grey edge of the sea
> and look seems most like me – being indeed my double
> ~~and yet (~~————) prove of all imaginable things
> the most unlike being my anti-self
> And here if these strange characters be understood
> (two lines unreadable, crossed out)
> and show me all I seek whisper it low
> ~~as though fear (~~————)
> as though he feared those birds that suddenly cry aloud
> make their momentary cries in the unbroken dark
> (two lines unreadable, crossed out)
> might carry it afar. here I carry it
> under the dawn, might carry it afar

    Ille's remonstrance becomes lines 63-66 in the final poem with minor but important changes. 'But wherefore', becomes the more direct 'Why should you', as Yeats succeeds in concretizing his diction. Later, the manuscripts of Yeats's early drafts indicate less archaism and stiltedness than we find in poems of the period of 'Ego Dominus Tuus'. The line 'by writing and rewriting' is completely dropped in revision, but its presence in the first draft shows how much the poem centres on the question of the creation of poetry. While Ille argues that self-conscious creation should be achieved by 'sedentary toil', by 'the imitation of the masters of the art', by writing and rewriting, Hic replies that for him finding a 'style' is not the primary goal of his struggle. 'Those,' he declares, 'who truly are most wise/own nothing but their blind stupefied hearts'. The truly wise must possess radical self-knowledge.
    The characters he makes in the sand, and which are 'traced' in the final poem, link 'Ego Dominus Tuus' directly to Yeats's magical experiments which led to his encounter with Leo Africanus and to

ASSERTION OF BELIEF TO CONFRONTATION OF THE ANTI-SELF

A Vision. As S. B. Bushrui[81] has pointed out in 'Yeats's Arabic Interests', Leo was only one of several Middle Eastern figures Yeats used. In *A Vision,* he describes an Arabic 'Judwali'[82] sect whose main activity was the attempt to penetrate reality by the making of 'diagrams' in the sand, When Yeats changes 'made' to 'trace' he seems to indicate that the patterns of reality which Hic/Ille and the Judwalis seek, are present and must be discovered by ritualistic activity.

Within the context of 'Ego Dominus Tuus', Hic in the draft rejects the masters of art and sedentary toil as ways to attain total consciousness and great art. Magical activity, making or tracing strange characters upon the sand is the path to self discovery through discovery of the anti-self. Hic, and Yeats, seek to be 'most wise' and own nothing but the 'blind stupefied heart'. In his earlier poetry, Yeats used the heart as a traditional symbol; it cried out, sang, wept. From this point, the heart is the place of deepest self-knowledge, the core of consciousness within the body from which comes all power. Since all true knowledge is in some sense secret knowledge for the magician/poet, the heart of the truly wise may be 'blind and stupefied', but not unconscious. Yeats said, in an essay written in the same year as 'Ego Dominus Tuus' was composed, that the body and the brain seem one in the man of energy and power,[83] and so, in ascribing the deepest self-knowledge to the heart, he is not suggesting that consciousness excludes the mind. For Yeats, consciousness, power, and divinity come from within the human body, from within consciousness, and so Hic and Yeats must seek their blind stupefied hearts through magical ritual if they are to be Dante-like, Christ-like figures.

'Ego Dominus Tuus' is a highly complex poem, especially in draft. Yeats is not rejecting the necessity for self-consciousness in matters of style when he has Hic reject Ille's question about his magical activity, for one of Yeats's major preoccupations in the draft is the finding of a style. He revised everything he ever wrote with increasing severity, and though this poem seems to have required less re-working than others, it clearly involved painful rethinking and reconstruction. For Yeats the bread of poetic toil is bitter but absolutely necessary to the totally conscious poet who would be responsible to his vision of reality and to his audience. Impulsive or half-conscious art such as Keats practiced will awaken dissipation and despair; Yeats seeks to play the role of prophet-poet, but not in the romantic mode. As Keats is relegated to the role of an ill-bred, snub nosed boy in this poem, so at this time was Yeats sifting his attitude toward the other Romantic poet who had earlier pleased him – Shelley. In 'Art and Ideas', he refers to Keats and Shelley as poets who 'intermixed into their poetry no elements from the general thought, but wrote out of the impression made by the world upon their delicate senses'.[84] They denied their inner selves and their responsibility to the common dream and wrote from sensation as Wordsworth wrote from moral maxims. Yeats sought to found his senses in total consciousness of himself and his connection to the *Anima Mundi,* denying no source of power. 'Why', he asked, 'should a man cease to be a scholar, a believer, a ritualist before he begin to paint or rhyme or to compose music, or why if he have a strong head should he put away any means of power?'

Hic and Ille do not contradict each other, being, as the draft clearly shows, interchangeable parts of Yeats's own personality. They are both Yeats, and both points of view are his. Consciousness must be founded in the self and requires knowledge of the anti-self, or opposite, but conscious style is important too. That Hic's statements become Ille's in the final version of the poem raises two possibilities: first, that at the point when he composed the draft, the Hic or 'him' side of his consciousness was more of a mask than the Ille or 'I' character was – that the worry over style was closer to him than the worry over discovery of himself; or, second, that both Hic and Ille were always equally parts of him but that timidity about expressing his magical beliefs and practices forced him to assign a 'him' the activity of summoning the anti-self. If the second possibility is correct, then by 1917 when 'Ego Dominus Tuus' was published, we may assume Yeats's courage had increased. But, most important, by 1912, Yeats was finally able to draft the first of his poems clearly to state the vital connection between consciousness, magic and the creation of poetry.

'Ego Dominus Tuus' is, like many of Yeats's subsequent poems, a poem about poetry and the poet. To trace or make the strange characters of the magical ritual which invokes the self through knowledge of the anti-self is complementary to tracing or making the characters of words on a page in the construction of a work of art. Poetry and Magic are rituals for Yeats, rituals which work toward penetration of the individual consciousness and the *Anima Mundi.* The role Yeats has assigned himself is that of Druidic prophet-poet, the man who through the practice of symbolic rituals achieves total consciousness and the power to penetrate the *Anima Mundi.* His responsibility is not moral nor aesthetic; he is the priest possessed of secret knowledge who provides man with his link to divinity, a divinity which is within all of us but directly accessible to the Druid-Poet. Yeats will, as the draft says, carry his consciousness and power far, always as the deliberate and invisible hypnotist, protecting his secret knowledge from Blasphemous men, as the poem tells us.

By 1912, Yeats was, despite his essentially private connections with magic and the occult, a solidly respectable figure in Dublin life, as the conjecture about offering him the Chair of English Literature at Trinity College evidences.[85] Yeats did not get the position, and probably did not really want it. Basically, as 'Ego Dominus Tuus' shows, Yeats was entering a new period of confidence and poetic production. After the dry years from 1903-1909, especially after 1912, believing that he had 'that common instinct, that common sense which is genius', and that he was finally possessed of that power which came because of 'something simple and impersonal' within him, he wrote some of his greatest poems, many of which would appear in *Responsibilities*, and at least one, 'The New Faces', dated 1912 in the manuscript,[86] which would appear in *The Tower*. Most critics have seen a basic shift in Yeats's work beginning with the poems of *Responsibilities,* while some would push the date of change backward to 1909 and some of the poems of *The Green Helmet and Other Poems*; these critics see *The Tower* as the full flowering of a style hinted at only since 1909-1914. But, clearly, a close examination of Yeats's work indicates that the shift began at the turn of the century and that the years to 1914 were of a single piece.

Surely by 1912 and 'Ego Dominus Tuus', Yeats had integrated his thought, his magic and his poetics. The voice we hear in *The Tower* is one for which he had consciously striven since 1900; for years he had been trying to muster all of the power he could in order to communicate his vision. It was not until *Responsibilities* that he fully used the invisible patterning he had practiced in his prose; but the poems from *The Green Helmet* begin to indicate what he will shortly practice so effectively.

While the twenty-one poems from *The Green Helmet* are not arranged in a clear pattern with each refracting and amplifying the statement of the other, they do work as a group to emphasize certain major themes and concerns which were to dominate the rest of his career. Only one poem in the group deals directly with death; none summons anyone to fairyland or a better world. Yeats began to be aware of himself as a public figure beset by 'theatre business' and the 'management of men',[87] and as a poet arrived at the point of being asked to praise his imitators.[88] Time, Truth, Love and Poetry dominate his thought in the volume, however, and the links he makes between these subjects are both stronger than before and infused by his sense of irony. While he had made connections between Poetry and Love before, and even suggested the devastating effect of Time upon both, as in 'Adam's Curse', never before has he turned his own youthful romanticism against himself with the wit and courage he begins to display in the poems from *The Green Helmet*. As a man 'Through with the lying days of my youth',[89] Yeats dismisses romantic love with an ironic sigh in 'A Drinking Song'.[90] He writes:

> Wine comes in at the mouth
> And love comes in at the eye;
> That's all we shall know for truth
> Before we grow old and die.
> I lift the glass to my mouth,
> I look at you, and I sigh.

As wine is a sensual and ephemeral quantity, so too is love a primarily physical and transitory experience. 'A Drinking Song' and 'The Coming of Wisdom with Time' are placed at the centre of the volume, immediately following 'The Fascination of What's Difficult', the three of them complementing each other's statements, and as if to reinforce his major themes, Yeats ends the volume with a poem about poetry followed by one about love. In 'All Things Can Tempt Me',[91] he says,

> All things can tempt me from this craft of verse:
> One time it was a woman's face, or worse –
> The seeming needs of my fool-driven land;
> Now nothing but comes readier to the hand
> Than this accustomed toil. When I was young,
> I had not given a penny for a song
> Did not the poet sing it with such airs
> That one believed he had a sword upstairs;
> Yet would be now, could I but have my wish,
> Colder and dumber and deafer than a fish.

Poetry is a craft from which he has been tempted by politics, by the theatre, by love in the form of a woman's face; he has been melodramatic and romantic in his poetic style; but now that verse comes so readily to him, he must reject the temptation to facility and superficiality. Yeats had reached a stage in his work where he saw himself in danger of writing with what Eliot calls 'a hollow and wasted virtuosity'[92] but he will not succumb. He seeks the

ASSERTION OF BELIEF TO CONFRONTATION OF THE ANTI-SELF

coldness which will enable him to focus all of his passion on his poetry.

'Brown Penny'[93] complements 'All Things Can Tempt Me', being linked by the image of the penny and by its rejection of Yeats's youthful attitudes. It is placed in the *Collected Poems* at the end of *The Green Helmet* section and immediately before *Responsibilities*. he writes:

> I whispered, 'I am too young'.
> And then, 'I am old enough';
> Wherefore I threw a penny
> To find out if I might love.
> 'Go and love, go and love, young man,
> If the lady be young and fair'.
> Ah, penny, brown penny, brown penny,
> I am looped in the loops of her hair.

We might read it as a wry love poem: love is worth only the common penny tossed in the first quatrain, and further limited by the caveat that the lady must be 'young and fair'. Once his choice is determined by the accident of a toss of a coin, the young man becomes lost in a labyrinth, as Yeats had been lost in *Hodos Chameliontos,* or as the poem states it, 'looped in the loops of her hair'.

By the second stanza, the wiser poet addresses the penny:

> O love is the crooked thing,
> There is nobody wise enough
> To find out all that is in it,
> For he would be thinking of love
> Till the stars had run away
> And the shadows eaten the moon.
> Ah, penny, brown penny, brown penny.
> One cannot begin it too soon.

Clearly, one cannot begin *loving* too soon: If one thinks about love, the 'crooked thing', he will be thinking until the end of time, 'Till the stars had run away/And the shadows eaten the moon'. Yeats wryly, but significantly, rejects passivity in the face of Time and change. By carefully placing the poem immediately before *Responsibilities*, Yeats suggests that as he should not have delayed loving, he should no longer delay writing the kind of poetry in which he believes.

The Green Helmet poems are marked by a sense of urgency, of time passing and of the need to act, to move with the whole earth which forever changes, 'Its flesh being wild'.[94] Seeking all knowledge, instead of the knowledge of his individual soul, he has avoided asserting in his poetry the vision he had integrated and which his prose long expressed. 'In dreams', he would write, 'begins responsibility'.[95] Yeats was ready to write of what he would call his *Responsibilities*.

NOTES

[1] One of the most noteworthy of the Millenialists was Robert Owen who founded communities both in Scotland and in New Harmony, Indiana, which were based upon Millenialist philosophy.

[2] W. B. Yeats, *Autiobiographies* (London: Macmillan, 1966), p. 300.

[3] *The Oxford Book of Modern Verse*, ed. W. B. Yeats (Oxford: Oxford University Press, 1936), pp. ix-xi.

[4] *Ibid.*, p. xiii.

[5] First printed in *Catholic Anthology* (1914-1915); reprinted in *The Wild Swans at Coole* (Dundrum: Cuala Press, 1917); appears in definitive edition (1956), p. 139.

[6] For a fuller discussion of Catullus see *Princeton Encyclopedia of Poetry and Poetics*, ed., Alex Preminger (Princeton, N. J.: Princeton University Press, 1965), p. 269.

[7] See Richard Ellmann, *The Identity of Yeats* (London: Faber and Faber, 1954), p. 254, for a note on Yeats's changes in the second stanza of 'The Scholars'. Ellmann does not read the poem as I do, but the changes he records support my reading.

[8] This opinion has been expressed recently in Harold Bloom, *Yeats* (New York: Oxford University Press, 1970), p. 107.

[9] See Richard Ellmann, *Yeats: The Man and the Masks* (London: Faber and Faber, 1949), p. 167. Ellmann asserts that the years 1903-1908 were a kind of void in Yeats's life and attributes the poet's problems to Maud Gonne.

[10] Unpublished paper read at Fall, 1972, SCMLA by George Harper. The idea is more fully discussed and documented in Harper's subsequently published *Yeats's Golden Dawn* (New York: Macmillan, 1974).

[11] W. B. Yeats, *Letters*, ed. Allan Wade (London: Hart Davis, 1954), pp. 339-340.

[12] *Ibid.*, p. 344.

[13] It may be significant to Yeats's attitudes in 1900 that his mother died in that year, but there is no particular support for this assumption.

[14] *Letters*, p. 343. Emphasis added.

[15] Actually, Yeats had begun to make the distinction between the effects of concrete and vague language when he did his work on Blake.

[16] *Letters*, p. 402.

[17] *Ibid.*, p. 403.

[18] W. B. Yeats, *Essays and Introductions* (London: Macmillan, 1961), p. 185.

ASSERTION OF BELIEF TO CONFRONTATION OF THE ANTI-SELF

[19] *Ibid.*, pp. 156-157.
[20] *Ibid.*, pp. 10-11. Emphasis added.
[21] From 'The Municipal Gallery Revisited', first printed in *A Speech and Two Poems* (Dublin: Cuala Press, 1937); reprinted in the definitive edition (1956), pp. 316-318.
[22] *Essays and Introductions*, pp. 206-210.
[23] *Letters*, p. 358.
[24] *Essays and Introductions*, p. 28.
[25] *Ibid.*, pp. 43-50.
[26] Wallace Stevens, *The Necessary Angel* (New York: Vintage, 1951), p. 35.
[27] *Essays and Introductions*, p. 49. (By 1924 when Yeats added a note to the essay, he was much more certain of his position. He wrote: 'I forgot that my 'subconsciousness' would know clairvoyantly what symbol I had really given and would respond to the association of that symbol. I am, however, certain that the main symbols (symbolic roots, as it were) draw upon associations which are beyond the reach of the individual "subconsciousness".'
[28] *Essays and Introductions*, p. 51.
[29] *Letters*, p. 434.
[30] Douglas Hyde, *A Literary History of Ireland* (London: T. Fisher Unwin, 1899), pp. 82-94. See also Virginia Moore, *The Unicorn* (New York: Macmillan, 1954), pp. 42-84, for another discussion of Druidic influence in Yeats.
[31] *Unicorn*, pp. 163 ff.
[32] *Ibid.*, p. 167. Moore has excerpted this material from the pamphlet, a copy of which is available in the collection of the Huntington Library.
[33] First printed in *The Monthly Review* (December, 1902); reprinted in *In The Seven Woods* (Dundrum: Dum Emer Press, 1903); appears in definitive edition (1956), pp. 78-79.
[34] Cf. *Letters*, p. 462.
[35] *Man and Masks*, pp. 154-156. See also Bloom's *Yeats*, pp. 164-166.
[36] See T. S. Eliot, *On Poets and Poetry* (London: Faber and Faber, 1957). Eliot cited 'Adam's Curse' in his tribute to Yeats which is reprinted in this collection of essays.
[37] See Richard Finneran, 'Yeats's Revisions in *The Celtic Twilight*, 1912-1925', *Tulane Studies in English*, 20 (1973), 97-105.
[38] *Man and Masks*, p. 169.
[39] See Una Ellis-Fermor, *The Irish Dramatic Movement* (London: Methuen, 1954), for a fuller discussion of the development of the Irish Theatre.
[40] W. B. Yeats, *Explorations* (London: Macmillan, 1962), p. 164. Lady Gregory was, of course, the first financier; Annie Horniman offered the use of the Abbey.
[41] *Ibid.*, pp. 124-140.
[42] *Ibid.*, pp. 153-154.
[43] *Ibid.*, p. 163.
[44] *Letters*, p. 466.
[45] *Ibid.*
[46] *Ibid.*, p. 469.
[47] *Ibid.*, p. 492.
[48] *Letters*, p. 495.
[49] *Ibid.*, p. 512.

50 *Ibid.*
51 *Autobiographies,* p. 583.
52 *Ibid.,* pp. 484-485.
53 See *Letters,* p. 499.
54 National Library of Ireland MS. 13,574.
55 *Autobiographies,* p. 461.
56 *Essays and Introductions,* p. 265.
57 See *Man and Masks,* pp. 188-196; and *Unicorn,* Chapters VI-VII.
58 *Autobiographies,* p. 461.
59 *Ibid.,* p. 468.
60 *Ibid.,* pp. 481-482.
61 *Ibid.,* p. 481.
62 *Ibid.,* p. 494.
63 *Ibid.,* p. 495.
64 *Essays and Introductions,* p. 339.
65 *Autobiographies,* p. 504.
66 *Essays and Introductions,* p. 330.
67 *Ibid.,* p. 310.
68 *Autobiographies,* p. 508.
69 *Essays and Introductions,* p. 336.
70 *Autobiographies,* p. 171.
71 *Ibid.,* p. 509.
72 *Ibid.,* p. 524.
73 *Ibid.,* p. 527.
74 *Essays and Introductions,* p. 256.
75 *Man and Masks,* p. 188.
76 See W. B. Yeats, *Memoirs,* ed., Denis Donoghue (New York: Macmillan, 1972); clearly, Yeats chose to end *Estrangement* with this passage because it was not the last one in the diary as the recently published *Memoirs* show.
77 *Man and Masks,* pp. 199-201. Ellmann assumed the poem was written in 1915, but manuscript evidence definitely indicates Yeats wrote it in 1912.
78 'Ego Dominus Tuus' appears in definitive edition (1956), pp. 157-159.
79 National Library of Ireland MS. 13,587.
80 *Essays and Introductions,* p. 339.
81 S. B. Bushrui, 'Yeats's Arabic Interests', in *In Excited Reverie,* ed., A. N. Jeffares and K. G. W. Cross (London: Macmillan, 1965), pp. 245-267.
82 W. B. Yeats, *A Vision* (London: Macmillan, 1962), p. 54.
83 See *Essays and Introductions,* pp. 343-345. Writing of John Shawe-Taylor, Yeats says: '. . . these men, copying hawk or leopard, have an energy of swift decision, a power of sudden action, as if their whole body were their brain.'
84 *Essays and Introductions,* p. 347.
85 See *Letters,* pp. 555 and 560; also see Joseph Hone, *W. B. Yeats 1865-1939* (London: Macmillan, 1967), pp. 249-251.
86 National Library of Ireland MS. 13,586 (1).
87 W. B. Yeats, 'The Fascination of What's Difficult', first printed in *The Green Helmet and Other Poems* (Dundrum: Cuala Press, 1910); appears in definitive edition (1956), pp. 91-92.
88 W. B. Yeats, 'To a Poet, Who Would Have Me Praise Certain Bad Poets, Imitators of His and Mine', first printed in *The Green Helmet and Other Poems* (Dundrum: Cuala Press, 1910); appears in definitive edition (1956), p. 92.

ASSERTION OF BELIEF TO CONFRONTATION OF THE ANTI-SELF

[89] W. B. Yeats, 'The Coming of Wisdom with Time', first printed in *The Green Helmet and Other Poems* (Dundrum: Cuala Press, 1910); appears in definitive edition (1956), p. 92.

[90] W. B. Yeats, 'A Drinking Song', first printed in *The Green Helmet and Other Poems* (Dundrum: Cuala Press, 1910); appears in definitive edition (1956), p. 92.

[91] First printed in *The English Review* (February, 1909); appears in definitive edition (1956), pp. 95-96.

[92] T. S. Eliot, *On Poetry and Poets* (London: Faber and Faber, 1957), p. 257.

[93] First printed in *The Green Helmet and Other Poems* (Dundrum: Cuala Press, 1910); appears in definitive edition (1956), p. 96.

[94] W. B. Yeats, 'At Galway Races', first printed in *The Green Helmet and Other Poems* (Dundrum: Cuala Press, 1910); appears in definitive edition (1956), p. 95.

[95] First printed in *Responsibilities: Poems and a Play* (Dundrum: Cuala Press, 1914); appears in definitive edition (1956), p. 98.

SELECTED BIBLIOGRAPHY

Selected Bibliography

Manuscript Sources

The manuscripts listed here are selected from the collection in the possession of the National Library of Ireland in Dublin. In listing them, I have maintained the form used in *Manuscript Sources for the History of Irish Civilization,* ed. Richard J. Hayes. Boston: G. K. Hall and Co., 1965.

Yeats, W. B.

Ms. 2662. 'Photostat' copies of letters from James Joyce to W. B. Yeats and to Lady Gregory from originals belonging to Michael B. Yeats and Major R. Gregory, 1902-1936.

——————.

Ms. 5460. Letters written by noted people in the Irish Press Controversy over the forged Casement Diaries by W. J. Maloney, together with two poems relating to the subject by W. B. Yeats.

——————.

Ms. 5918. A Collection of Autograph and typed letters by W. B. Yeats, including letters to John O'Leary and Count Plunkett, dealing with literary affairs, to G. R. Barnes of the B.B.C. in connection with a broadcast of his poetry and to Cyril Fagan of the Irish Astrological Society, 1889-1938.

——————.

Ms. 5925. Autograph letters from J. B. Yeats and W. B. Yeats to John O'Leary dealing mainly with Art and Literature, 1887-1897.

——————.

Ms. 8763. Typescript with many extensive manuscript variants and one complete Ms. copy by W. B. Yeats, of his play The Hourglass.

——————.

Ms. 8771. Scenario and various versions in typescript and Ms. by W. B. Yeats of his play Purgatory.

——————.

Ms. 10,854. Thomas McDonagh papers: 34 letters mainly to Thomas McDonagh including two by him and two by W. B. Yeats, 1903-1906.

Yeats, W. B.
Ms. 13,095. 'Photostat' copy of title page and half title of a copy of W. B. Yeats's The Tables of the Law with a note by Seamus O'Sullivan identifying James Joyce as the 'young man' noted by Yeats in his prefatory note.

Ms. 13,568. Notes and other materials by Miss Horniman, W. B. Yeats and others toward the establishment of a Mystical Celtic Order.

Ms. 13,569. Fragmentary notes on Mystical topics including one folder in the hand of W. B. Yeats.

Ms. 13,570. W. B. Yeats's Occult diary and notebook, 1889.

Ms. 13,571. Typescripts and corrected galleys by W. B. Yeats of his introductions to plays.

Ms. 13,574. Notes by W. B. Yeats on Irish Gods and legends. In two hard-backed notebooks.

Ms. 13,575. Notes by W. B. Yeats on Lady Gregory's Visions and Belief[s] and text (ms. and typescript) of his essay on Swedenborg, Mediums . . . one hard-backed note-book and three folders.

Ms. 13,576. Note-book of W. B. Yeats begun April 7, 1921, containing Vision material, diary entries and including theme for 'Among School Children'.

Ms. 13,578. 'Rapallo note-book A' (lettered A on front fly leaf, D on front cover): notebook of W. B. Yeats containing rewritten sections of A Vision, including comments on The Cat and the Moon, passages of The Player Queen, prose entitled The Irish Censorship, a letter about Wagner.

Ms. 13,579. 'Rapallo note-book B': note-book of W. B. Yeats containing materials for A Vision.

Yeats, W. B.
Ms. 13,580. 'Rapallo note-book' (diary) (finished June or

July, 1929): note-book of W. B. Yeats containing diary of thoughts, Vision materials, poems (drafts, etc.) from The Winding Stair and Words for Music Perhaps, including Cracked Mary (later Crazy Jane) poems.

———. Ms. 13,581. 'Rapallo note-book (diary)' (Folder 3 headed 'Dublin August 1929'): note-book of W. B. Yeats containing, *inter-alia*, many versions of poems in The Winding Stair, including Byzantium.

———. Ms. 13,582. 'Rapallo note-book E': note-book of W. B. Yeats containing 'Resurrection'; work on A Vision; drafts of Words upon the Window Pane.

———. Ms. 13,586. W. B. Yeats's drafts, revisions, etc. of poems published in Responsibilities, with one item from The Tower.

———. Ms. 13,587. W. B. Yeats's drafts, revisions, etc., of poems published in The Wild Swans at Coole.

———. Ms. 13,588. W. B. Yeats's' revisions, etc., of poems published in Michael Robartes and the Dancer.

———. Ms. 13,589. W. B. Yeats's drafts, revisions, etc., of poems published in The Tower with some rejected poems.

———. Ms. 13,590. W. B. Yeats's drafts, revisions, etc., of poems published in The Winding Stair.

———. Ms. 13,591. W. B. Yeats's drafts, revisions, etc., of poems published in Words for Music Perhaps.

———. Ms. 13,592. W. B. Yeats's drafts, revisions, etc., of poems published in Last Poems.

Selected Published Works of W. B. Yeats

Yeats, W. B. *John Sherman and Dhoya.* London: T. Fisher Unwin, 1891.

———. *The Tables of the Law and The Adoration of the Magi.* London: Elkin Mathews, 1904.

Yeats, W. B. *Collected Works.* 8 vols. Stratford-on-Avon: Shakespeare Head Press, 1908.

——————. *Reveries Over Childhood and Youth.* New York: Macmillan, 1916.

——————. *Wheels and Butterflies.* London: Macmillan, 1934.

——————. *Wheels and Butterflies.* New York: Macmillan, 1935.

——————. *On the Boiler.* Dublin: Cuala Press, 1939.

——————. *The Variorum Edition of the Poems,* ed. Peter Allt and Russell K. Alspach. New York: Macmillan, 1957.

——————. *Collected Poems.* 2nd ed., London: Macmillan, 1950.

——————. *Collected Poems.* Definitive Edition, New York: Macmillan, 1956.

——————. *Letters to John O'Leary and His Sister,* ed. Allan Wade. New York: Macmillan, 1953.

——————. *Letters to Katherine Tynan,* ed. Roger McHugh. New York: Macmillan, 1953.

——————. *W. B. Yeats and T. Sturge Moore: Their Correspondence,* ed. Ursula Bridge. London: Macmillan, 1953.

——————. *Letters,* ed. Allan Wade. London: Hart-Davis, 1954; New York: Macmillan, 1955.

——————. *Senate Speeches,* ed. Donald R. Pearce. Bloomington, Indiana: Indiana University Press, 1960.

——————. *Essays and Introductions.* London: Macmillan, 1961.

——————. *Explorations.* London: Macmillan, 1962.

——————. *Mythologies.* London: Macmillan, 1962.

——————. *Selected Poems and Two Plays,* ed. M. L. Rosenthal. New York. Macmillan, 1962.

——————. *A Vision.* London: Macmillan, 1962.

——————. *Selected Criticism,* ed. A. Norman Jeffares. London: Macmillan, 1964.

——————. *Autobiographies.* London: Macmillan, 1966.

——————. *Collected Plays.* London: Macmillan, 1966.

——————. *The Variorum Edition of the Plays,* ed. Russell K. Alspach. London: Macmillan, 1966.

SELECTED BIBLIOGRAPHY

Yeats, W. B. *John Sherman and Dhoya,* ed. Richard J. Finneran. Detroit, Michigan: Wayne State University Press, 1969.

———. *Ah, Sweet Dancer: W. B. Yeats and Margot Ruddock,* ed. Roger McHugh. New York: Macmillan, 1970.

———. *Uncollected Prose,* Vol. I, ed. John P. Frayne. New York: Columbia University Press, and London: Macmillan, 1970.

———. *Memoirs,* ed. Denis Donoghue. New York: Macmillan, 1972.

Works Edited and Introduced by Yeats and by Yeats with others

Blake, William. *Works,* ed. E. J. Ellis and W. B. Yeats. 3 vols., London: Bernard Quaritch, 1893.

———. *Poems,* ed. W. B. Yeats. London: Routledge and Kegan Paul, Ltd., 1905.

Gregory, Lady Augusta. *Visions and Beliefs in the West of Ireland,* with Essays and Notes by W. B. Yeats. 2nd ed., Gerrards Cross, Buckinghamshire, England: Colin Smythe, 1970.

The Oxford Book of Modern Verse, ed. W. B. Yeats. Oxford: Oxford University Press, 1936.

The Ten Principal Upanishads, put into English by Shree Purohit Swami and W. B. Yeats. London: Faber and Faber, 1937.

Villiers de l'Isle-Adam. *Axel,* trans., H. P. R. Finsburg; preface by W. B. Yeats. London: Faber and Faber, 1952.

Yeats, W. B. *Irish Fairy and Folk Tales.* New York: Modern Library, n. d. (1888).

Further Letters and Materials Related to Yeats's Poetry

A Concordance to the Poems of W. B. Yeats, ed. Stephen Maxfield Parrish. Ithaca, New York: Cornell University Press, 1963.

Russell, George. *Some Passages from the Letters of AE to W. B. Yeats.* Dublin: Cuala Press, 1936.

Wellesley, Dorothy. *Letters on Poetry from W. B. Yeats to Dorothy Wellesley.* London: Oxford University Press, 1964.

Yeats, J. B. *Letters to His Son and Others, 1869-1922,* ed. Joseph Hone. London: Faber and Faber, 1944.

Yeats, J. B. *Further Letters,* selected by Lennox Robinson. Dublin: Cuala Press, 1920.

──────. *Passages from the Letters of J. B. Yeats,* selected by Ezra Pound. Dublin: Cuala Press, 1917.

Selected Works Related to the Study of Yeats

Abrams, M. H. *The Mirror and the Lamp.* New York: W. W. Norton and Co., Inc., 1953.

Adams, Hazard. *Blake and Yeats: The Contrary Vision.* New York: Russell and Russell, 1955.

Berryman, Charles. *W. B. Yeats: Design of Opposites.* New York: Exposition Press, 1967.

Beum, Robert. *The Poetic Art of William Butler Yeats.* New York: Frederick Unger, 1969.

Blackmur, F. P. *Form and Value in Modern Poetry.* New York: Anchor, 1957.

Blavatsky, H. P. *The Secret Doctrine.* Point Loma, Calif.: Theosophical Publishing Co., 1910.

──────. *Isis Unveiled.* Los Angeles, California: Theosophy Co., 1925.

Bloom, Harold. *Yeats.* New York: Oxford University Press, 1970.

Bornstein, George. *Yeats and Shelley.* Chicago: University of Chicago Press, 1970.

Bradford, Curtis. *Yeats at Work.* Carbondale and Edwardsville, Illinois: Southern Illinois University Press, 1965.

Clark, David R. *W. B. Yeats and the Theatre of Desolate Reality.* Dublin: Dolmen Press, 1965.

Crowley, Aleister. *The Confessions of Aleister Crowley,* ed. John Symons and Kenneth Grant. New York: Bantam, 1971.

Donoghue, Denis. *William Butler Yeats.* New York: Viking, 1971.

Dume, T. L. *W. B. Yeats: A Study of His Readings.* Philadelphia: University of Pennsylvania Press, 1950.

Eddins, Dwight. *Yeats: The Nineteenth Century Matrix.* University, Alabama: University of Alabama Press, 1971.

SELECTED BIBLIOGRAPHY

Eglington, John (William Kirkpatrick Magee). *Irish Literary Portraits*. London: Macmillan, 1935.

Eliot, T. S. *The Sacred Wood*. London: Methuen, 1950.

——————. *On Poetry and Poets*. London: Faber and Faber, 1957.

Ellis-Fermor, Una. *The Irish Dramatic Movement*. London: Methuen, 1954.

Ellmann, Richard. *Yeats, The Man and the Masks*. London: Faber and Faber, 1949.

——————. *The Identity of Yeats*. London: Faber and Faber, 1954.

——————. *Eminent Domain*. New York: Oxford University Press, 1967.

Engleberg, Edward. *The Vast Design: Pattern in W. B. Yeats's Aesthetic*. Toronto: University of Toronto Press, 1964.

Evans-Wentz, W. Y. *The Tibetan Book of the Dead*. New York: Oxford University Press, 1957.

Garab, Arra M. *Beyond Byzantium: The Last Phase of Yeats's Career*. Dekalb, Illinois: Northern Illinois University Press, 1969.

Guha, Naresh. *W B. Yeats: An Indian Approach*. Calcutta: Jadaupur Press, 1968.

Grossman, Allen R. *Poetic Knowledge in the Early Yeats: A Study of Wind Among the Reeds*. Charlottsville, Va.: University of Virginia Press, 1969.

Harper, George Mill, *Yeats's Golden Dawn*, London: Macmillan, New York: Barnes & Noble, 1974.

Henn, T. R. *The Lonely Tower*. London: Methuen, 1950.

Hone, Joseph. *W. B. Yeats 1865-1939*. London: Macmillan, 1967.

Hough, Graham. *The Last Romantics*. London: Methuen, 1947.

Hyde, Douglas. *A Literary History of Ireland*. London: T. Fisher Unwin, 1899.

Ishibashi, Helen. *Yeats and the Noh*. Dublin: Dolmen Press, 1965.

Jeffares, Norman. *W. B. Yeats, Man and Poet*. 2nd ed., London: Routledge and Kegan Paul Ltd., 1962.

Joyce, James. *The Critical Writings*, eds. Ellsworth Mason and Richard Ellmann. New York: Viking, 1959.

Jung, C. G. *Memories, Dreams, Reflections,* ed. Aniela Jaffe; trans. Richard and Clara Winston. New York: Alfred A. Knopf, 1965.

Kermode, Frank. *Romantic Image.* London: Routledge and Kegan Paul, 1957.

Levi-Strauss, Claud. *The Raw and the Cooked: Introduction to a Science of Mythology,* trans. John and Doreen Weightman, Vol. I. New York: Harper and Row, 1969.

MacLiammoir, Michael and Eavan Boland. *W. B. Yeats and His World.* New York: Viking, 1971.

MacNeice, Louis. *The Poetry of W. B. Yeats.* London: Faber and Faber, 1941.

Marcus, Phillip L. *Yeats and the Beginnings of the Irish Renaissance.* Ithaca and London: Cornell University Press, 1970.

Meester, Marie de. *Oriental Influences in the English Literature of the Nineteenth Century.* Heidelberg: C. Winter, 1915.

Melchiori, Giorgio. *The Whole Mystery of Art.* London: Routledge and Kegan Paul, 1960.

Miller, J. Hillis. *Poets of Reality: Six Twentieth Century Writers.* Cambridge, Mass.: Harvard University Press, 1966.

Moore, John Reese. *Masks of Love and Death: Yeats as Dramatist.* Ithaca and London: Cornell University Press, 1971.

Moore, Virginia. *The Unicorn.* New York: Macmillan, 1954.

Orel, Harold. *The Development of William Butler Yeats: 1885-1900.* Lawrence, Kansas: University of Kansas Publications, 1968.

Oshima, Shotaro. *Yeats and Japan.* Tokyo: Hokuseido Press, 1965.

The Oxford Classical Dictionary, ed. N. G. L. Hammond and H. H. Scullard. 2nd ed., Oxford: Clarendon Press, 1970.

Parkinson, Thomas F. *Yeats, Self-Critic.* Los Angeles: University of California Press, 1951.

—————. *W. B. Yeats: The Later Poetry.* Berkeley and Los Angeles: University of California Press. 1964.

Perloff, Marjorie. *Rhyme and Meaning in the Poetry of Yeats.* The Hague and Paris: Mouton, 1970.

SELECTED BIBLIOGRAPHY

Princeton Encyclopedia of Poetry and Poetics, ed. Alex Preminger. Princeton, N.J.: Princeton University Press, 1965.

Rajan, Balachandra. *W. B. Yeats.* London: Hutchinson University Library, 1969.

Richards, I. A. *Principles of Literary Criticism.* 2nd ed., London: Routledge and Kegan Paul, 1926.

Ronsley, Joseph. *Yeats's Autobiography: Life as Symbolic Pattern.* Cambridge, Mass.: Harvard University Press, 1968.

Rudd, Margaret. *Divided Image: A Study of William Blake and W. B. Yeats.* London: Routledge and Kegan Paul, 1953.

Saul, George Brandon. *Prolegomena to the Study of Yeats's Poems.* Philadelphia: University of Pennsylvania Press, 1957.

—————. *Prolegomena to the Study of Yeats's Plays.* Philadelphia: University of Pennsylvania Press, 1958.

The Secret of the Golden Flower, trans. Richard Wilhelm. London: Kegan Paul, Trench, Trubner and Co., Ltd., 1932.

Seiden, Morton Irving. *William Butler Yeats: The Poet as Mythmaker, 1865-1939.* East Lansing: Michigan State University Press, 1962.

Stallworthy, Jon. *Between the Lines: Yeats's Poetry in the Making.* London: Oxford University Press, 1963.

—————. *Vision and Revision in Yeats's Last Poems.* London: Oxford University Press, 1969.

Stevens, Wallace. *The Necessary Angel.* New York: Vintage, 1956.

Suzuki, Daisetz Teitaro. *The Essence of Buddhism.* 2nd ed., Kyoto: Hozokon Press, 1968.

Thompson, William Irwin. *The Imagination of an Insurrection: Dublin, Easter 1916.* New York: Oxford University Press, 1967.

Torchiana, Donald T. *W. B. Yeats and Georgian Ireland.* Evanston, Illinois: Northwestern University Press, 1966.

Unterecker, John. *A Reader's Guide to W. B. Yeats.* London: Thames and Hudson, 1959.

Ure, Peter. *Towards a Mythology: Studies in the Poetry of W. B. Yeats.* Russell and Russell, 1967.

Ure, Peter. *Yeats.* London: Oliver and Boyd, 1963.

Ure, Peter. *Yeats, the Playwright.* London: Routledge and Kegan Paul, 1963.

Vendler, Helen Hennessy. *A Vision and the Later Plays.* Cambridge, Mass., and Oxford: Harvard University Press, 1963.

Wade, Allen. *W. B. Yeats.* London: Soho Bibliographies, 1951.

Waley, Arthur. *The No Plays of Japan.* London: Allen and Unwin, 1921.

Whitaker, Thomas. *Swan and Shadow.* Chapel Hill: University of North Carolina Press, 1964.

Wilson, F. A. C. *W. B. Yeats and Tradition.* London: Methuen, 1958.

——————. *Yeats's Iconography.* London: Methuen, 1960.

Winters, Yvor. *The Poetry of W. B. Yeats.* Denver: A Swallow, 1960.

Zimmer, Heinrich. *Myths and Symbols in Indian Art and Civilization,* ed. Joseph Campbell. Princeton, N.J.: Princeton University Press, 1946.

Selected Collections of Essays

In Excited Reverie: Critical Essays on W. B. Yeats, ed. A. N. Jeffares and K. G. W. Cross. London: Macmillan, 1965.

The Dolmen Press Yeats Centenary Papers, ed. Liam Miller. Dublin: Dolmen Press, 1968.

The Integrity of Yeats, ed. Dennis Donoghue. Cork: The Mercier Press, 1964.

The Permanence of Yeats, ed. James Hall and Martin Steinmann. New York: Macmillan, 1950.

'W. B. Yeats: Critical Perspective', *Southern Review,* V, No. 3, n. d. (Summer, 1969), 831-949.

W. B. Yeats, ed. D. E. S. Maxwell and S. B. Bushrui. Ibadan:

W. B. Yeats, 1865-1939: Centenary Essays on the Art of W. B. Yeats, ed. D. E. S. Maxwell and S. B. Brushrui. Ibadan: Ibadan University Press, 1965.

The World of W. B. Yeats: Essays in Perspective, ed. Robin Skelton and Ann Saddlemyer. Victoria, B.C.: University of Victoria by the Adelphi Bookshop Ltd., 1965.

Yeats: A Collection of Critical Essays, ed. John Unterecker. Englewood Cliffs, N.J.: Prentice-Hall, 1963.

SELECTED BIBLIOGRAPHY

Yeats: Last Poems, ed. Jon Stallworthy. London: Macmillan, 1968.

'Yeats and the 1890s', *Yeats Studies,* I (1971).

Yeats and the Occult, ed. G. M. Harper. London: Macmillan. Toronto: Macmillan of Canada, 1975.

Selected Periodical Essays

Adams, Hazard. 'Survey of Criticism', *Texas Studies in Language and Literature,* III (1962), 439-451.

——————. 'Yeats, Dialectic and Criticism', *Criticism,* 10 (1968), 185-199.

——————. 'The W. B. Yeats Collections at Texas', *Library Chronicle of the University of Texas,* VI (1962), 53-58.

Atkins, Anselm. 'The Vedantic Logic of Yeats's "Crazy Jane",' *Renascence,* XIX (1966), 37-40.

Ayling, Ronald. 'W. B. Yeats on Plays and Players', *Modern Drama,* IX (1966), 24-38.

Beum, Robert. 'Yeats's Octaves', *Texas Studies in Language and Literature,* III (1961-62), 89-96.

Bradford, Curtis. 'The Order of Yeats's *Last Poems*," *Modern Language Notes,* LXXVI (1961), 515-516.

——————. 'The Speckled Bird: A Novel by W. B. Yeats', *Irish Writing,* 31 (Summer, 1955), 9-15.

——————. 'Yeats and Maud Gonne', *Texas Studies in Language and Literature,* III (1961-62), 452-474.

Brogunier, Joseph. 'Expiration in Yeats's Last Plays', *Drama Survey,* V (1966), 24-38.

Byars, John A. 'Yeats's Introduction of the Heroic Type', *Modern Drama,* VIII (1966), 409-418.

Ellmann, Richard. 'Ez and Old Billyum', *Kenyon Review,* XVIII (1966), 470-495.

Finneran, Richard J. 'Yeats's Revisions in *The Celtic Twilight,* 1912-1925', *Tulane Studies in English,* 20 (1973), 97-105.

Harper, George Mills. 'All the Instruments Agree: Some Observations on Recent Yeats's Criticism', *Sewanee Review,* LXXIV (1966), 739-754.

Houghton, W. E. 'Yeats and Crazy Jane', *Modern Philology,* XL (1966), 316-329.

Hurwitz, Harold M. 'Yeats and Tagore', *Comparative Literature,* XVI (1964), 55-64.

Iskander, Fayes. 'Yeats and Cocteau: Two Anti-Romantics', *Cairo Studies in English,* 1963-66, pp. 119-135.

Jeffares, Norman, 'Yeats as a Modern Poet', *Mosaic,* II, No. 4 (Summer, 1969), 53-59.

Kain, Richard M. 'W. B. Yeats: Centenary Studies and Tributes', *Southern Review,* n. s. 3 (1967), 742-756.

Kelleher, John V. 'Yeats's Use of Irish Materials', *Tri-Quarterly,* No. 4 (1965), 115-125.

Knights, L. C. 'W. B. Yeats: The Assertion of Values', *Southern Review,* VII (1941-42), 426-441.

Matthiessen, F. O. 'The Crooked Road', *Southern Review,* VII (1941-42), 455-470.

Mise, Raymond. 'Yeats's Crazy Jane Poems', *Paunch,* No. 25 (1966), 18-30.

O'Driscoll, Robert. 'The Tables of the Law: A Critical Text', *Yeats Studies,* I (1971), 87-119.

Rose, M. G. 'An Interview with Anne Butler Yeats', *Modern Drama,* VII (1964-65), 299-308.

Saul, George Brandon. 'Coda: The Verse of Yeats's Last Years', *Arizona Quarterly,* 17 (1961), 63-68.

Spender, Stephan. 'The Influence of Yeats on Later English Poets', *Tri-Quarterly,* No. 48 (1965), 82-89.

Stock, A. G. '*A Vision* (1925 and 1937)', *Indian Journal of English Studies,* I (1960), 38-47.

Stucki, Yasuko. 'Yeats's Drama and the No: A Comparative Study in Dramatic Theories', *Modern Drama,* IX (1966) 101-122.

Wall, Richard J. and Roger Fitzgerald. 'Yeats and Jung: An Ideological Comparison', *Literature and Psychology,* XIII (1963), 44-52.

Warshausky, Sidney. 'Yeats's Purgatorial Plays', *Modern Drama,* VII (1964), 278-286.

Witt, Marion. 'Yeats's "Song of the Happy Shepherd",' *Philological Quarterly,* XXXII (1953), 1-8.

Index

Abbey Theatre: 100, 119, 126.
  See Irish National Theatre
Adams, Hazard, 37
Aherne, Owen, 85, 86, 87, 95, 96, 128
Africanus, Leo, 129, 130, 133, 136
Alchemy, 25, 40, 85, 86
Anglo-Irish, the, 54, 55, 56, 57, 66
Anima Mundi, 7, 26, 45, 79, 91, 92, 100, 101, 134, 138
Apocalypticism, 85, 100, 107, 108
Apollo, 111
Art, 99, 112, 126, 127

Battle, Mary, 90, 91, 93
Beardsley, Aubrey, 95
Bennett, Alan, 122
Berkeley, Bishop, 55, 57
Bhagavad Gita, 124
Black Magic, 25, 73
Blake, William, 7, 21, 37-48, 53,
Blackmur, R. P., 72
Blake, William, 7, 21, 37-48, 53, 57, 66, 74, 79, 115
Blavatsky, Madame Helena, 9, 22, 23, 24, 25, 27, 32, 37, 39, 57, 58
Bloom, Harold, 38, 46
Bridges, Robert, 54
Buddha, 123
Buddhism, 7, 24, 122, 123
Burke, Edmund, 55, 57
Bushrui, S. B., 137
Butler, Samuel, 95

Cabbalism, 7, 22, 27, 32, 37, 39, 45, 57, 70, 79, 90, 95, 97, 101, 117, 118, 123, 126
Calvinism, 69
Catholic Ireland: compared to Protestant Ireland, 70-71
Catholicism, 97, 101
Catullus, 108, 109
Celtic Mystical Order: 54, 89. *See* Irish Mystical Order

Celtic tradition, 57, 62, 66, 69, 71, 81, 82, 101, 117
Chatterjee, Mohini, 17, 22, 23, 40
Chavannes, Puvis de, 100
Christ, 82, 123, 133, 137
Christianity, 83, 100
Coleridge, Samuel Taylor, 65
Columcille, 68, 77*n*, 117
Connolly, James, 94, 101
Consciousness: linked to art, 17, 99, 116, 124, 125, 137, 138
Crowley, Aleister, 109, 110, 117, 125

Dance: as metaphor, 85
Dante, 132-33, 135, 137
DaVinci, Leonardo, 56
Demon est Deus Inversus, 121
Dionysus, 111
Dowden, Edward, 20
Dowson, Ernest, 20, 59, 95, 97
Drama, 120
Dreaming back, 80
Drugs, 99
Druidh: defined, 116
Druids, 67, 82, 83, 116, 117, 138, 139
Dublin Hermetic Society, 16, 22
Duffy, Sir Charles Gavan, 59, 60, 63

Eastern Thought, 16, 20, 21, 40, 65, 124
Eliot, T. S., 66, 96, 140
Elitism, 113
Ellis, Edwin, 37, 39, 50*n*, 59
Ellis-Yeats Edition: 37-51 *passim*; *See* Quaritch Edition
Ellmann, Richard, 11, 13, 16, 24, 25, 59, 72, 79, 86, 87, 92, 110, 118, 119, 128
Emerson, R. W., 97
Emmanuel, 101, 107
Emmet, Robert, 94

161

INDEX

English tradition, 62
Eugenics, 114
Evil, 66, 68, 73, 74, 82, 97

Fantasy, 110
Folklore, 21, 57, 65, 75, 92, 93, 115
Form: Yeats's concern for, 61-62

Gaelic Literature, 57
Golden Dawn, the, 7, 25, 81, 91, 109, 122
Gonne, Maud, 41, 59, 94, 119
Goethe, J. W. von, 122
Great Memory: connection to magic, mythology, poetry, 15
Great Memory, 114, 115, 116. *See* Anima Mundi
Great Mind, 125
Great Soul, 117
Gregory, Lady I. A., 58, 63, 64, 65, 89, 92, 93, 94, 100, 114, 119
Guha, Naresh, 33n, 34, 35

Harper, George, 34n, 109
Hera, 88
Hermetic Thought, 66
History, 97
Hone, Joseph, 11
Horniman, Annie, 119
Horace, 108
Humour, 68, 70
Hyde, Douglas, 20, 59, 65, 76-77n, 116, 117

I Ching, 7
Imagination, 59, 110
Incarnation, the, 124, 125
Indian Philosophy and Thought: 17, 25, 29, 30, 32, 37, 53, 66. *See* Eastern Thought
Ireland: 17, 102; Yeats's relationship to, 54, 56; in Yeats's poetry, 49, 53; source for Yeats's subject matter, 17, 53, 54, 32; linked to poetry and magic, 17, 19
Irish Folklore, 53, 64, 65, 66, 69, 70, 74, 79, 82, 88, 90, 95, 101, 124
Irish legends and History, 23, 62, 82, 89
Irish Literature: 60, 62; publication scheme, 59

Irish Literary Society, 59
Irish Mystical Order, 42, 43, 81, 88-89, 95
Irish Mythology: 21, 53, 57, 64, 65, 71, 72, 74, 75, 79, 100, 101; connected to Buddhism, 122, 123
Irish National Theatre: 89, 93, 95, 119, 120. *See* Abbey Theatre
Irish Nationalism, 17, 64, 94, 101
Irish Renaissance, 62, 75
Irish poetry and magic, 53
Irish Senate, 56-57
Irony, 60, 68, 69, 70, 75, 108, 127, 140

Jeffares, A. N., 11
John, Augustus, 121
Johnson, Lionel, 11, 20, 59, 95, 97
Joyce, James, 55, 64
Judwali Sect, 137
Jung, C. G., 6. 102n

Keats, John, 134, 135, 137, 138
Kenner, Hugh, 12

Language: Yeats's concern for, 47, *A Literary History of Ireland*, by 48-49, 54, 89, 93, 102n, 113, 116
Hyde, D., 116, 117
Lucifer, 121

MacBride, Major, 94, 101, 119
Macleod, Fiona: 114. *See* William Sharp
Magic: 5, 12, 18, 40, 62, 70, 74, 75, 81, 95, 98, 101, 102, 112, 114, 117, 123; definition, 110; distinguished from mysticism, 5; as power, 53, 58, 125; and poetry, 8, 11, 21, 32, 37, 40, 41, 53, 54, 82, 88, 101, 115, 130, 138; linked to Yeats's idea of Ireland, 17; and unity of culture and being, 20-21
Magical rituals, 22, 88, 92, 136
Magician; 22, 25, 116, 133, 134, 137; defined, 5
Mallarmé, Stéphane, 87, 100
Mandalas, 89, 112, 115
Mannin, Ethel, 41
Martyn, Edward, 89

INDEX

Mathers, MacGregor, 7, 22, 25, 26, 27, 32, 37, 39, 81, 89, 91, 92, 95, 100, 101, 109, 110, 112, 117, 125
Mask, 124, 126, 129
Memory of the race: 92; *See* Anima Mundi
Metempsychosis, 117
Millenialism, 107
Milton, John, 18
Mirandola, Pico della, 25
Moore, George, 89
More, Henry, 25, 95
Moreau, Gustave, 100
Mystical Celtic Order: 25. *See* Golden Dawn
Mystagogues, 110
Mystic: 92; defined, 5
Mysticism; 5, 48, 85, 86, 99, 101, 112, 117, 125; in Catholicism, 71, 103n; Yeats's struggle against, 87-88
Mythology, 5, 57, 81, 101, 112, 125

National Literary Society, 59
Nietzsche, F., 111
Neo-Platonism, 25, 72
Newman, Cardinal, 97
Numerological symbols, 115

Occult, 5, 32
O'Brien, Conor Cruise, 55, 94
O'Grady, Standish, 20
Ogham, 83-84
O'Leary, John, 6, 17, 53, 60, 61, 63, 64, 90, 92, 93
O'Shea, Katharine, 61
Order of the Alchemical Rose, 85, 87
Owen, Robert, 142n

Paganism, 71
Parkinson, Thomas, 33n
Parnell, Charles Stewart, 53, 54, 55, 58, 61, 90
Pater, Walter, 44, 45, 61, 108
Pearse, Patrick, 94
Personality, 97
Pitt, William, 121
The Playboy of the Western World, 121-122
Platonism, 72, 116. *See* Neo-Platonism

Poet, 79, 81
Poetic form, 49, 74, 83, 111
Poetry, 56, 61, 80, 107, 108, 112, 140
Pollexfen, George, 89, 90, 91, 101
Pollexfen, William, 12-13, 15
Pope Leo X, 129
Porphyry, 72
Pound, Ezra, 127
Pre-Raphaelitism, 39
Protestant Ireland, 126
Psychical Research, 17

Quaritch Edition: 57, 58. *See* Ellis-Yeats Edition
Quaternity, 42, 43, 44, 46
Quinn, John, 111, 121

Reincarnation, 23
Rhymers' Club, 59, 61, 62, 83, 95, 99, 107, 108, 109, 120
Rhys, Ernest, 20
Robartes, Michael, 85, 86, 87, 95, 96, 129
Rosicrucian Magician, 128
Russell, George (AE), 12, 16, 20, 23, 48, 73, 92, 99, 111, 121, 125

Saint Martin, L. C. de, 99
Saint Patrick, 83
Seances, 17
The Secret of The Golden Flower, 6, 7
Secret knowledge, 31, 124
Sexuality, 15, 47
Shakespear, Olivia, 6, 42
Sharpe, William: 95. *See* Fiona Macleod
Shaw, G. B., 95, 96, 97
Shelley, P. B., 5, 21, 58, 138
Sidhe, the, 15, 66, 70, 73, 74, 84
Socrates, 123
Spiritualism, 128, 129
Stella Matutina, 34n, 118
Stevens, Wallace, 44, 48, 116
Style, Yeats's concern for, 84
Supernatural, the (also supernormal), 12, 15, 18, 112, 113, 126
Swift, Jonathan, 55
Symbols, 6, 7, 47, 100, 101, 115, 116 124
Symons, Arthur, 20, 59, 122

INDEX

Synge, John M., 20, 64, 68, 71, 89, 95, 100, 114, 121, 122, 126, 127
Synchronicity, 91, 102*n*

T'ai I Chin Hua Tsung Chih, 6, 7, 26
Taoism, 6
Taylor, John F., 61
Telepathy, 26, 88, 89, 90, 115
Thaumaturgy, 124
Theosophy, 7, 22, 32, 37, 53, 57, 66, 70, 74, 79, 122
Time, as theme, 31, 32, 118, 139
Timon, 121
Tone, Wolfe, 93
Tynan, Katharine, 17, 31, 39, 56, 64

Usna, 82
Unity of Being, 96
Unity of Culture, 20, 53, 58, 93, 97

Vedantism: 22; Yeats's rejection of, 30
Verlaine, Paul, 20, 95, 100
Victoria's Jubilee, 93
Villon, F., 121
Violence, 93-94
Virgil, 108
Visions, 74, 75, 90, 92, 99, 100, 101, 110, 114, 123, 142

Wellesley, Dorothy, 5
Whitman, W., 97
Wilde, Lady, 66
Wilde, Oscar, 20, 64, 95, 96, 97
Will, 124
Will and Mask, 97
Wilson, F. A. C., 72
Witchcraft, 113
Wordsworth, W., 138

Yeats, John Butler (Yeats's father), 13
Yeats, Susan Pollexfen (Yeats's mother), 13
Yeats, William Butler, works by:
'Adam's Curse', 118, 119, 140;
'The Adoration of the Magi',
82, 85, 88; 'All Things Can Tempt Me', 140, 141; 'Among School Children', 18, 27, 81; *Autobiographies*, 19, 37, 53, 60, 73, 79, 81, 95, 96, 100, 108, 112; 'The Autumn of the Body', 111 'The Balloon of the Mind', 14; 'Brown Penny', 141; 'The Child and The State', 57; 'The Choice', 98; 'The Celtic Element in Literature', 11, 112; *The Celtic Twilight*, 66, 67, 68, 70, 72, 73, 74, 75, 82, 119; *Collected Works* (1908), 119; 'The Coming of Wisdom with time', 140; *Crossways*, 7, 21, 49; 'The Death of Synge', 126; *Deirdre*, 82, 119, 122; *Discoveries*, 99, 123; 'A Drinking Song', 140; 'Ego Dominus Tuus', 8, 128-39 *passim*; *Estrangement*, 122, 123, 125, 126, 129; 'The Fairy Doctor', 31; 'The Fascination of What's Difficult', 140; 'The Fiddler of Dooney', 79-80; 'First Principles', 121; *The Golden Helmet*, 122; *The Green Helmet and Other Poems*, 139, 140, 141; 'Hopes and Fears for Irish Literature', 61-62; 'Hodos Chameliontos', 7, 40, 79-105 *passim*, 141; *The Hour Glass*, 119; *Ideas of Good and Evil*, 111, 119; 'In Memory of Major Robert Gregory', 103*n*; *In The Seven Woods*, 118, 119; 'An Indian Song', 29; 'Into the Twilight', 67; 'Ireland After Parnell', 64, 73, 75; 'Ireland and the Arts', 114; *Irish Fairy and Folk Tales*, 21, 53, 65; *Is the Order of the R. R. and A. C. to Remain a Magical Order?*, 117; 'The Island of Statues', 29; 'Jealousy', 30, *John Sherman*, 95; 'Kanva on Himself', 29; *The King's Threshold*, 119; 'The Lake Isle of Innisfree', 21; 'Magic', 8, 114, 115, 116; *Memoirs*, 79, 101; *Michael Robartes and the Dancer*, 19; 'Mohini Chatterjee', 23;

INDEX

Yeats, William Butler, works by (continued) *Mythologies*, 81; 'The Necessity of Symbolism', 37, 40; 'The New Faces', 139; *On Baile's Strand*, 119; *On The Boiler*, 114; *Oxford Book of Modern Verse*, 107-108; *Per Amica Silentia Lunae*, 115, 128; *The Player Queen*, 122; *The Pot of Broth*, 119; *Poems (1895)*, 30, 81, 119; 'Quatrains and Aphorisms', 29; *Responsibilities*, 8, 118, 139, 141, 142, *Representative Irish Tales*, 21; *Reveries Over Childhood and Youth*, 7, 12, 13, 14, 15, 19, 74, 81; *The Rose*, 49, 79; 'Rosa Alchemica', 81, 85, 87, 88; 'The Sad Shepherd', 28; *Samhain (1904)*, 119; 'The Scholars', 108; 'The Second Coming', 26; *The Secret Rose*, 54, 79, 81, 82, 86, 87, 88, 89, 98, 100, 101, 107; 'The Secret Rose', 87; 'The Seeker', 31; *The Shadowy Waters*, 119; 'She Who Dwelt Among the Sycamores', 30; 'The Song of The Happy Shepherd', 27-28; 'The Stirring of the Bones', 100; *Stories of Red Hanrahan*, 'Symbolism in Painting', 47; 'Tables of the Law', 81, 82, 85, 87; 'Tales From the Twilight', 68; 'Time and the Witch Vivien', 31; 'To Ireland in the Coming Times', 49; *The Tower*, 19, 139; 'The Tragic Generation', 95, 96, 99; *The Trembling of the Veil*, 19, 20, 21, 54, 58, 89, 95; *A Vision*, 6, 19, 80, 81, 96, 115, 124, 128, 137; *The Wanderings of Oisin*, 21; 'What is Popular Poetry?', 113; 'The White Birds', 80; 'William Blake and His Illustrations to the *Divine Comedy*', 37, 46; 'William Blake and the Imagination', 37, 46; *The Wild Swans at Coole*, 19; *The Wind Among the Reeds*, 67, 79; *The Winding Stair*, 98

Young Ireland, 59

Zodiac, 122